Playgrounds that work

Creating Outdoor Play Environments for Children Birth to Eight Years

Pauline Berry

Pademelon Press

Acknowledgments

I would like to thank Jenny Allen, Louise Angus, Polly Butler, Kay Colmer, Betty Fox, Robyn Geisler, staff and parents, Jenny Hocking, Angela Norris, Merylyn Rowe, Jen Tieman and her staff, and all of those staff members who took the time to provide me with information on what they would find useful in a book such as this.

The photographs in this book were taken at the Margaret Ives Children's Centre in Norwood, South Australia. Many thanks to the staff and families for their cooperation.

Many of the stories in this book have come from experiences I have had when working with staff and committees who have been redeveloping their centre's playground.

A special thanks to Elizabeth Dau and Jill Huntley.

First published in February 2001 by
Pademelon Press
PO Box 6500, Baulkham Hills BC 2153
New South Wales, Australia

Berry, Pauline (Pauline M.).
Playgrounds that work: creating outdoor play environments for children birth to eight years.

Bibliography.
Includes index.
ISBN 1 876138 10 6.

1. Play environments. 2. Playgrounds. 3. Play environments—Planning. 4. Play environments—Design and construction. 5. Play. I. Title.

711.558

Editing and indexing by Forsyth Editorial Services
Cover design and page composition by ID Studio, Sydney
Printed in Australia by Gillingham Printers Pty Ltd

This book is dedicated to Jim whose support and encouragement was invaluable.

Table of contents

Introduction

I assume that the readers of this book are aware of the value of play. I do not want to spend too much time on what has already been written about by so many before me. Rather, I wish to focus on the more practical things that will assist staff and committees in providing appropriate outdoor learning environments for young children. The emphasis of this book is more on learning environments rather than those designed for recreational use only.

Before anyone can design outdoor play environments for young children it is important that they are aware of the differing needs of children in the various age groups and the stages of their development. What would be a favourite pastime for one age can be of no interest to another and interest and curiosity is what motivates children to explore their environment.

To provide such an environment one needs to have an understanding of child development and of children's play behaviours in the outdoors, how they move through a space, the value of certain play features, how children use them and the importance of placement.

The main reason for this book comes from a strong desire to provide children in the early childhood years to the age of eight with exciting, stimulating and challenging outdoor environments. Many of the areas covered are the result of questions asked and problems faced by early childhood centres wishing to improve their outdoor play environments.

My interest in playgrounds began when I was appointed director of a preschool in the beautiful leafy foothill suburb of Tea Tree Gully, Adelaide. The playground had several large gum trees and outside the fence was a park full of native trees and shrubs that attracted numerous native birds. Inside the fence was uninteresting, except for high up in the treetops, where birds chattered freely.

A metal climbing structure was in the centre of the playground with chunky tan bark underneath and around the structure. Children continually walked around the outside of the tan bark, seldom venturing onto the bark to use the structure.

At the side of the tan bark was a tall gum tree with a small, low platform around the trunk. This platform had to be cut away from the tree regularly to prevent it from ringbarking the tree as it grew. When there was enough space between the tree trunk and the platform, children would post shoes and other important objects that we, as staff, found almost impossible to retrieve. The platform was too small to place furniture on it to encourage children's dramatic play and their favourite pastime was to run round and round the tree holding onto the trunk as they went.

The playground was sloped at one end and previous developers had retained the top level area with wooden railway sleepers and terraced the sloping area. This actually cut the bottom section off for the children as it interrupted the traffic flow from the top to the bottom of the playground. It was then that I became aware of the need to consider the child traffic flow in playgrounds and how the placement of features and materials, as well as the design of buildings, affects the way children move around a playground.

The metal climbing structure was removed and so too was the chunky tan bark — this area was one of the few areas not in shade. A watering system was installed and a hardy lawn was planted. Another platform was added to one side of the existing platform; one large enough to take a table and some chairs or a dolls bed. Movable shade cloth could be placed over the top. On the other side a narrow jetty-like platform was built so that children could go fishing from the sides or, if we placed a chair and a steering wheel at the end, it could become a truck or bus.

Several changes were made to provide access to the lower level of the playground. A digging area was established at the bottom level to provide a reason for the children to go down to that level. We designed three different ways to get to the bottom. In the first the sleepers were removed and at one end a sloping compacted sand path, suitable for small wheelbarrows and carts, led down to the digging area. In the second, moss-covered rocks were positioned in the centre so that children could meander through the rocks and down to the bottom area. One rock had a smooth rounded top that reminded the children of a whale, another became their horse or a motorbike as it was upright with a flat section that two children could sit on, and a cluster of low smooth rocks became the home of a princess.

The third way down was a series of pebble-filled ponds with tree trunk edges that children could climb up and over when dry. The top pond could be used separately for children to observe the small river stones and how they change colour when wet, or they could use it to find out what might float or sink. Each pond could overflow into the next until the water reached the bottom level. Children would dig their own creek around the gum trees at the bottom. With the children we planted young trees in the corner of the playground to utilise the water and we encouraged the children to dig their creeks so that the water would reach the area of the young trees.

We also enlarged the existing sandpit, extending it around a tree. To make sure the tree didn't die, we built a low wooden platform around it to protect the trunk. We had been told that if we raised the level around the base of the tree it could kill it; we could only raise the level of soil or sand gradually over time. As the children used the platform, sand slowly filtered through and the tree survived. This platform turned out to be a most successful addition to the sandpit — it doubled as a seat in the middle of the sandpit, it became a table for baskets of sand toys, an oven to cook cakes and a place where planks could be placed to slope down into the sand for trucks and cars.

Since I have been working with staff and committees in early childhood centres I have often found an imbalance in the types of play opportunities available to children, particularly play equipment that caters for some of the children's physical needs but little else. More thought needs to be given to children's needs and play behaviour when choosing equipment and other play features. One piece of equipment does not suit all ages and every situation, and one piece of equipment can never be 'the complete educational experience'. Equipment must be age-appropriate — structures designed for older children can be a safety hazard for younger ones.

Playgrounds have become an expensive business, with more and more fixed structures being erected in playgrounds; structures that often have little appeal to children. We seem to have lost sight of what children like to do. When asking adults where they liked to play as children, it nearly always involved nature, climbing trees, secret places, building cubbies, damming creeks, making mud pies, catching tadpoles and so on.

I can remember how much fun I had as a child in a nearby park. I climbed the old fig tree that hung over the creek, dropped stones into the water and watched the ever-increasing ripples, caught tadpoles in the creek and watched them grow into frogs. What fun it was when I returned the frogs to the creek, watching them jump and where they went.

Sometimes a friend and I built a cubby under the tree by brushing the soil with a leafy branch until it was flat and hard to form a floor.

I used to play 'chasings' with friends up and down the low-grassed mounds and hide in the bushes beside the creek.

Unfortunately today, young children do not have the same freedom. Families do not always have time to take their children to parks and it is not safe for them to go alone. This is why we have an added responsibility to recreate some of these more natural features in our playgrounds.

In a world where much of the natural environment has been replaced by cement drains instead of creeks, manicured gardens to look at but not touch, and where cleanliness is preferable to messy play, children need to feel free to explore and discover for themselves the wonders of nature and make sense of the world around them. We need a society of people who will care for our planet and be sensitive to issues that could destroy the little we have left. Many forests and natural bushlands have already disappeared to make way for development. How will our children learn to value the beauty and wonder of nature unless we, as early childhood educators, provide them with a rich environment where they feel free to wallow in its wonder?

> Nature deserves a prominent place in the environment for children.
> (Rijnen 1993, p. 24)

When planning an early childhood playground one must remember it is an important part of the educational program. Children's developmental needs must be catered for with play features and experiences that suit their wide range of needs, skills and interests.

An early childhood playground is not like a public playground, which is designed for recreational use, it is part of the learning environment and as such must cater for long-term use. It must be flexible so that it can change according to the children's needs, it must be challenging but safe according to the age range and skills of the children, and it must be interesting for the curious, creative and adventurous children.

Children need unstructured time, freedom to explore, discover, have adventures and fun with their peers. They need time and space to have quiet times, messy times and creative times, times to construct, to pretend and to solve problems, as well as time and space to engage in physical and social play. They need an outdoor environment that facilitates learning.

The developmental stages listed in Chapters 4–7 are chosen specifically as they are suitable to be fostered by outdoor experiences.

A section titled 'suggestions for staff' follows each age section. The suggestions are in no way comprehensive but are purely ideas based on children's developmental needs. Staff need to be aware of each child's needs so they can provide appropriate experiences to match those needs. It is important to establish goals for children in the outdoors and programming is essential. However, this book does not cover programming details.

It is important for the readers of this book to understand that the concept designs in the book have been included to demonstrate how some schools and centres have developed their playgrounds to incorporate many of the ideas discussed. These plans are garden designs, not professionally drawn, to demonstrate how centres can present their own simple plans to ensure that the centres have maximum input into the final layout.

All designs need to be individually planned as each location has differing variables that will affect the design. These variables are outlined in Chapters 2 and 3. The play features and concepts are not intended to be used as a recipe but as ideas to inspire and motivate people working for and with children in their endeavours to create an exciting and stimulating environment for children.

chapter 1 Play features for young children

This chapter covers a variety of play features with information on the experiences the features may provide; how children of different ages might use the features; and the developmental areas the features promote. It also covers placement in the playground. Information is also provided on research findings, where available, of children's use of equipment.

The chapter is divided into three sections:

1. *Fixed play areas* covers play features that need to be constructed to suit the needs of the children, and the space available in the centre.
2. *Fixed play equipment* covers manufactured play equipment that needs to be installed as fixtures in the playground.
3. *Natural play features* introduces the idea that not all play features need to be manufactured — they can be part of the landscape. For example, children can obtain climbing experience on a mound and engage in dramatic play in natural bush cubbies.

Very little information is included on construction as this information is available from the Australian Standards. The relevant standards are:

- Playgrounds and Playground Equipment Part 1, Development, Installation, Inspection, Maintenance and Operation (AS/NZS 4486: 1997); and
- Playground Surfacing (AS/NZS 4422: 1996).

These standards can be obtained from:

Standards Office
Telephone 1300654646

or downloaded from the Internet:

www.standards.com.au

or can be found in a very useful book titled *Playground Safety*, published by the New South Wales Health Department. Copies can be obtained from:

Kidsafe NSW
C/– The New Children's Hospital
PO Box 3515
Parramatta NSW 2124
Telephone (02) 9845 0890

chapter 1

Fixed play areas

Sandpits

Sand is one of the most popular play mediums for children in the early childhood years. It can be used in a variety of ways — from the simple feel of it as it runs through the fingers, to the filling and emptying of containers, and then to complex constructions. All sandpits must have some damp sand or have easy access to water. Sandpits without some damp sand are not as popular because children cannot mould the sand, or construct anything. They find it very frustrating trying to work with dry sand and it often leads to inappropriate behaviour such as throwing or kicking the sand. Also dry sand blows away in the wind and into children's eyes.

Early research by Steele and Nauman (1985) found that sand was the preferred activity regardless of what else was available to babies aged 10–20 months. They preferred large open sandpits, whereas older toddlers preferred the smaller cosy ones, especially when playing alone. Research in 1994 of children aged four to five years (Berry, 1994) showed sand play to be the most popular activity with more children spending longer periods of time in the sand area than in any other available activity (see Appendix 2).

Children can play with sand on their own, parallel to others or cooperatively with others. As they near five years of age the groups become larger and the constructions become more complex. Social skills and language skills develop through sharing the sand area. Children communicate with others when working together constructing roads, building bridges and dams or making cakes or witch's brew as part of their dramatic play.

Most of the activities in the sandpit exercise the upper body. The use of tools in the sandpit requires the coordination of many muscles. Digging holes in damp sand with hands instead of tools strengthens the muscles in the hands.

Problem-solving skills develop as children grapple with the questions of how to build a bridge in the sand, how to work with a child who keeps 'taking my spade' or how to lay plumbing pipes in the sand so that the water will flow through to the other end.

Additional materials need to be available to children in the sand to extend the possibilities for exploration and discovery. Balance-scales in the sand allow children to experiment with wet and dry sand — 'Which is heavier?', 'How much more do I have to put on one side to balance the scales?'. Natural materials, such as leaves, flowers, twigs and stones, can be collected by the children from the immediate environment. Staff can have collections of shells, sponges, seed-pods and pine cones readily available. Boxes of sand toys such as buckets, spades, rakes, sieves, saucepans, cake tins, wheelbarrows, plumbing pipes, pulleys, cars and trucks can be placed in the sandpit area. It is recommended that different types of materials are made available from time to time to change the play possibilities.

Figure 1.1 shows children working together in the sand. Sandpits need to be large to accommodate all the children who want to use the area at the same time. In many play areas there seems to be a

igure 1.1 Children digging in a sandpit

dolls, and create settings for their dramatic play. This sanded area can also be used for children practising long-jumps or as an area for curriculum extension work.

It is better if sandpits are not positioned too close to a centre's building. All children using sand will track sand from the pit on their clothes, their feet and in pockets. Parents are often heard to say that their children are gradually bringing home the whole sandpit!

When constructing a sandpit it is advisable to have the sandpit at ground level to reduce the possibility of children tripping over edges. Non-slip pavers around the edge will allow staff and children to sweep the sand back into the sandpit. It is not necessary for children to have access to a sandpit on all sides. It is preferable to reduce the access and exits from the sandpit by planting low bushy shrubs along some of the sides, wooden sleeper seats/ledges on another side, or low flat rocks that will double as seats or tables. These will provide more interesting and cosy areas for the children to play, as well as reducing the spill of sand. Paved openings between the garden beds will help direct the child traffic flow towards other areas of interest.

If the sandpit is large enough a low central table of decking will provide a space to make cakes, run trucks down a plank, store sand toys or be used as a seat. It is useful if the deck is low enough for children to use while sitting in the sandpit.

comfortable number that an area can accommodate. Usually for preschool children it is between five and eight, but, in a sandpit, 15 preschool children will happily play together, especially if the sand is damp or if there is water available in or nearby (for example, a bucket of water or a water feature emptying into the sandpit).

Children over five attending school will use a sandpit in a similar way to preschool children and it is important that they have this opportunity. A shallow sanded area as well as a sandpit provides a place for school-age children to make tracks for their cars, and

If the sandpit is in a windy position, screening plants on the side of the prevailing winds will protect the area and reduce the amount of sand blowing away. The best way to reduce the amount of sand blowing away is to keep the sandpit damp.

Sandpits are often placed under trees as there is shade readily available. However, this can present problems with the roots and leaves of the trees in the sand. An area planned for a sandpit needs to be excavated between about 800 mm to 1 m deep for children over three and a half and about 400 mm for younger children. To excavate to these depths means disturbing any tree roots often resulting in damage to the trees. Another problem that can arise is tree roots looking for moisture may intrude into the sand. It is preferable to construct a sandpit away from large trees and erect a pergola over the area to provide shade.

A sandpit needs to be generously shaded to ensure children are protected from ultraviolet rays. This is an area where children spend long periods of time and are vulnerable to severe skin damage. (For further discussion please see the section on shade in this chapter and Appendix 4.)

If the centre has trouble with cats fouling the sand, the sand must be disinfected and covered. Covers for sandpits need to allow rain, sun and air to pass through into the sand to keep it healthy. Shade cloth held down by tyres, wooden blocks or some other heavy item is sufficient. Cats do not like shade cloth as their claws get caught up in the net.

If the centre has problems with vandals or deposits of needles and syringes, a more substantial cover needs to be designed. If a permanent system of anchoring the shade cloth is installed, the anchors must not present a hazard to children, nor should the cover become an occupational health and safety issue for staff.

Although children with disabilities will use sandpits in a similar way to children without disabilities, children with physical disabilities must be catered for specifically. If there are children in wheelchairs in the centre, a raised sandbox section must be added to the sandpit to allow children in wheelchairs to have access to the sand and still be able to interact with able-bodied children as they play.

Water features

Water is an essential play medium. Without it many of the outdoor activities we provide for our children lose their appeal and the children are robbed of very valuable learning opportunities. However, it is most important in our dry country that used water is recycled. If a centre is going to install a water feature, that water must not be channelled down a drain but used either in a sandpit, a digging area or to water plants.

Water changes the composition of sand and soil. It makes a considerable difference to the time children spend playing with sand or soil, and it extends the play and learning possibilities. Playing with water is a very soothing pastime. Children can experiment with objects to see what floats and sinks; water changes or highlights the colour of many objects; it can be frozen and melted, and it evaporates.

All sandpits and digging areas should have a tap close by so that children have access to water. However, a hose is often attached to these taps creating a trip hazard for children. The other disadvantage is that there is always one child who claims ownership of the hose and restricts other children from using the water. Staff need to police the hose continually to ensure that every child has a turn. A fixed water feature overcomes these problems and gives staff more control over when it is appropriate to use water and the volume of water used.

Many preschools and schools have had water features installed. Some have 'creeks' running down a slope into a sandpit or a digging area. Children have great fun solving the problem of how to dam up the water. They need to work cooperatively to build a dam of stones to reduce the flow of water down the creek.

Water-pumps have proven to be a problem as they block with sand. Usually the water is supplied by a tap, which can be turned on and off when staff are in the area. A vandal-proof tap is useful as the top of the tap can be removed, which acts as a deterrent to vandals who may decide to 'flood' the centre. It also prevents children from turning the tap on or increasing the amount of water flow.

Another type of water feature is a shallow pond placed on the edge of the sandpit. The pond can be constructed of flat rocks on the top suitable for sitting on and lined with brushed cement. In the centre of the base is a drain and plug. When the plug is removed water drains through an overflow pipe into the sandpit, and when the plug is in, the water flows through several crevices in the rocks into the sandpit creating a waterfall effect. If the overflow pipe is a standard PVC plumbers' pipe then extra pipes can be attached by the children during their play to direct water to other parts of the sandpit.

Water in early childhood centres and schools does present a safety issue. Young children can drown in a small amount of water and water lying around can create a health hazard. *All water must be closely supervised* and staff members must never leave an area without emptying all contained water — small unattended brothers and sisters of children attending the centre could fall into the water. Fish ponds need mesh over the top for safety reasons as well as acting as a deterrent to birds wishing to fish in the pond.

If staff and parents are reluctant to install a creek or pond, a water feature that does not hold a volume of water but is purely a sloped brushed cement apron that feeds water into the sandpit on a wide front is an option. When water trickles into a sandpit on a wide front it allows several groups of children to gain access to the water at the same time.

The most simple water feature is a tap on the edge of the sandpit with a smooth flat rock placed under the tap that slopes towards the sand. In this instance always use a vandal-proof tap.

A fish pond, or one for frogs or water plants is well worth considering in school playgrounds. They need to be positioned in a quiet area away from the active areas where seats and shade trees encourage children to gather. Children can study the life cycle of creatures that live in water and learn how to respect and care for them. The pond can provide a quiet place to sit and observe or an opportunity for groups of children to gather and interact.

Digging areas

Digging in soil provides a very different activity to that of digging in sand. Soil offers a certain amount of resistance to the spade whereas sand offers very little. Children stand up to dig soil and they use metal spades or very strong plastic spades. Often they need to put their foot on the head of the spade to help it cut through the soil. The pushing against this resistance helps strengthen the muscles in the arms and legs and requires the coordination of the whole body. It requires a lot of energy to dig soil and it is this vigorous physical activity that can release tensions and bring children down from a 'high' when they become very excited. Figure 1.2 shows a generous sized digging area where children have space to explore and discover.

Children can make exciting discoveries when digging in soil; they can find worms, slaters, roots of weeds, interesting stones or treasure and the occasional shell or bone. These are all discoveries that can be extended by watchful staff who can make connections with reference books and props that will extend the interest into other areas.

Figure 1.2 Digging soil

Working in the digging area encourages children to socialise and solve problems together and allows for group construction of channels and rivers, and the laying of pipes as they may have seen in nearby streets.

When water is added the soil makes wonderful mud pies:

- Sarah's preschool had been discussing healthy foods with children in an attempt to encourage them to bring fruit for morning tea rather than chips. Linda the teacher had set up the digging area with water, rubber boots, hard hats and wheelbarrows and placed a table next to the area with scone trays, bowls and cooking utensils in a container nearby. Long waterproof aprons that would cover the children's clothing hung on a stand next to the table. A group of children had been making channels, laying pipes and directing water through the pipes into a hole they had dug in the digging area when Sarah (4 years, 9 months) and Justin (4 years, 6 months) took a bowl each out of the container and asked the children if they could have some mud.

The mud was scooped out by one of the children with a plastic soup ladle.

Sarah and Justin returned to the table with their mud and proceeded to spoon mud into a scone tray and place it on a chair in the sun to 'cook'.

Sarah was mixing some mud in a bowl when another child ran up to the table and asked them what they were doing. 'We're making chocolate mousse,' said Sarah. 'Its good for you, you know!' ●

Digging areas in the past have been small plots of hard soil, impossible to dig, and uninteresting to all who pass by. Children need a reason to dig. Interesting large rocks with no sharp edges, or a fallen tree trunk placed in the centre of the area, will provide children with the opportunity to dig around, under, or in between the rocks. They also provide a place to sit and watch other children dig or rest from their hard work.

Successful digging areas are often messy, and not what visitors need to see as they enter the centre for the first time. They need to be positioned as far away from the front gate as possible and in an unused corner or area not previously utilised. The digging area needs to be in a partially shaded place, large enough to accommodate at least four or five children at a time with room to construct on a large scale. Sandy loam, or old sand from the sandpit dug into the existing soil to lighten it up, will enable children to dig successfully. The area can be defined by bricks, smooth rocks or timber edging or not have any edging at all, depending on the area available and the size of the playground.

As **metal spades** are the most suitable tool for digging there are safety issues that must be addressed before children can play in this area. The area must be well supervised by a staff member, children need to wear rubber boots to protect their feet from the spades, no spades should be raised higher than the waist, hard hats need to be worn to represent road workers and their dress, but at the same time protect the children's heads from an unruly spade. This is an area that tends to be dominated by boys, so it is important for staff to encourage girls into the area as well.

This activity is most suited to children over three-and-a-half years old who can adhere to the rules of working in a digging area. If parents are unhappy about mud on the children's clothes, waterproof pants or overalls could be made and become part of the 'workers' uniform. A low table next to the digging area allows for extension activities such as weighing 'dinosaur bones', sorting treasures, or even making mud pies or 'chocolate mousse'.

Adjuncts to a digging area include: water, plumbing pipes, trucks, buckets, pulleys, metal or hard plastic spades, rakes, wheelbarrows, bricks, timber planks, blocks of wood, cooking utensils, leaves and flowers.

Bike tracks and pathways

Bike tracks and paths for bikes, ride-on toys and push–pull toys need to be positioned where they do not cut across the play of other children. Ideally they are best placed on the side of a playground with access to the verandah or door of the storage shed. They need to be wide enough for two bikes to pass each other, have a hard smooth surface, and be interesting enough to hold the attention of the children as they play.

How the path is designed depends upon the age group using the path. Very young children who have just learnt to walk often use the push–pull toys to support them as they walk. These children have difficulty turning corners so a path with wide curves is best and it needs to be close to the building so that they feel safe. As they become more confident they need a path that passes plants of different textures, colours and smells. The path needs to be partially in shade with trees that have leaves that rustle in the wind and attract birds. Bench seats in the general area give staff the opportunity to watch and support the children when needed without being too close.

As the children become more skilled in their bike riding they need more interesting things around them to explore. For example, areas where they can park their bikes and visit another area or become engaged in dramatic play where they ride their bikes to work, school or to the shops, or areas that can be set up as service stations or shops. Large road signs, such as STOP, START, GO, TRAINS, will enrich the play as would make-shift petrol pumps.

As children become proficient bike riders they look for new challenges, which often involves the bike in front. They enjoy crashing into another bike, upsetting the child who is on the bike and watching the result of the crash, or they like to cause a traffic jam so that no-one can move. Bikes are expensive toys and the maintenance on the bikes is constant, so it is best to avoid the crashes.

Before the children begin to use the bikes inappropriately it is important to create a section of track with inbuilt challenges, like slight rises where they have to push hard to get up the rise, archways to ride through, perfumed plants either side that brush against the children as they ride, and rumble strips that create a bumpy ride. If there are many age groups using the playground all with different stages of riding ability, it is useful to have a simple section and a complex section to cater for all the needs.

Many children who have reached the age of four to five have bikes at home. It is important to survey the families and find out if all the children have bikes. If they do, the space might be better utilised for some other activity.

Have you noticed that when you have a certain number of bikes all in good working order there is always one that everyone wants, either the one with the silver bit on the back or the red one?

Animal settings

Animals fascinate children. Nursing a guinea pig or rabbit is a very special experience for young children. The keeping of animals in early childhood centres provides children with the opportunity to learn about the needs of other creatures. They learn about life cycles, what the animals eat and the need to handle the creatures gently and caringly. They can take on the responsibility of feeding the animals and cleaning out their enclosures, with adult guidance. Children with low self-esteem become more confident through having the opportunity to befriend an animal and learn about that particular animal's needs and characteristics.

Children often have their first experience of death when a pet dies and this experience helps them learn to deal with the concept of death:

● It was a sad day when we arrived at kindergarten to discover Thumper, our white rabbit, had died overnight. All the children had the opportunity to stroke Thumper and tell him how sad they were that he had died.

We decided to bury Thumper in our flower garden. The children helped dig the hole and made crosses at woodwork class to place on his grave. There was a discussion amongst the children about Thumper going to Heaven. About a half an hour later a small group of children asked if they could 'dig a hole and see if Thumper had gone to Heaven yet?'

This experience was one the children never forgot and many of the parents took the opportunity to talk to their children about death and dying. The centre lent some of the parents story books such as *I'll Always Love You* (Wilhelm, 1985) and *Lifetimes* (Mellonie and Ingpen, 1983) to help in family discussions. ●

Animals kept outdoors can be in danger of being hurt by vandals or predators, such as foxes. It is important to have a safe place for any animals kept on the premises. Find out about the regulations regarding the keeping of pets before you buy one. If the requirements are too complicated, or no-one on the staff is prepared to take final responsibility for the animal, it is preferable to have an enclosure for visiting animals that can be used during the day when the opportunity arises.

Amphitheatres

Amphitheatres are places where children can sit and socialise, a quiet place to read books or watch other children nearby, a place to watch a performance, an area for dramatic play or an outdoor classroom.

The size and the placement depends on the age of the children who are likely to use it, and how it will be used. The floor of the amphitheatre can be grassed or have a hard surface, depending on the use. Wheelchairs need a paved floor and space on one end to accommodate the wheelchair.

All amphitheatres must be well shaded (see the section on shade in this chapter).

Babies who are mobile and toddlers will use a mini-amphitheatre, comprising of several railway-sleeper steps in a 'U' shape in the side of a grassy mound. Here they will sit for a short time, or climb or clamber up and over the other side.

Children under five need a small two-tiered amphitheatre that allows eye contact with other children sitting opposite them. It can be used for small group activities such as story reading, fruit time or, if equipped with props and furniture, as a place for dramatic play. Children can also use this area as a watching place so they can watch other children at play before deciding to join in.

Figure 1.3 Amphitheatre

Figure 1.3 shows an amphitheatre that would be good for children three to five years.

It is most important that this structure is positioned close to the building. Amphitheatres placed away from the building will not be used unless a staff member constantly sits in the area. Sometimes staff members cannot see any value in amphitheatres but this is often because their experience has been with amphitheatres that are positioned incorrectly:

● At one time I was appointed to a preschool with a well-established playground. The amphitheatre was to one side of the building with the main play area on the other. It was seldom used. Children sitting in the amphitheatre could not see children at play on the other side of the playground and must have felt isolated. Unless an adult sat in the area it was not used. Another centre, however, had an identical amphitheatre, but positioned so that it was at the end of the verandah. Children used to bring dress-ups, books and outdoor building blocks into the area and it was constantly used. ●

Amphitheatres in schools need to be large and have several tiers so that they can accommodate a whole class. English, dance, drama and human movement classes can be held in the area; they can be used as an official or unofficial meeting place or a place where students can eat during recesses and lunches.

Amphitheatres need to be places that can be used by all the school community — students and staff as well as parents who can sit and talk to other parents while waiting for children at the end of the day.

Many amphitheatres are constructed of timber railway sleepers, which make ideal seating, however it is important that regular maintenance checks are made to ensure that there are no splinters (if there are, the timber needs to be sanded).

Gazebos

These structures tend to lend themselves to quieter areas, surrounded with plants and having either fixed seating and a central table or movable furniture. They can be used as an outdoor classroom, or a meeting place. Any fixed seating must be at a comfortable height for the users. A fixed table in the centre does tend to restrict the use; for example, bringing in additional furniture could be difficult. If one was placed in a school playground it would certainly be used as a meeting place as school-age children need a place to meet friends and generally 'hang out'. A winding path from the classroom to the gazebo through a sensory garden would have great appeal.

Verandahs

Verandahs are extremely useful in early childhood settings. They provide shelter from the sun and the rain. Often during winter children are unable to play outdoors and with everybody inside for a whole session, the noise level can become unbearable. It is important that there is a place where children can go, where there is fresh air and protection from the rain.

Many centres have installed heavy-duty clear plastic blinds along the edges of verandahs. These protect children from the rain and wind and still allow the light through. Canvas blinds or awnings should be installed for the summer when the ultraviolet rays are at their peak in the middle of the day. Verandahs need plants nearby for shade or adjustable awnings that swing out and extend the shade area.

In child-care centres it is useful to fence off part of a verandah and place a carpet and cushions on the floor for the less mobile babies to enjoy the outdoors without the danger of being walked on. It is preferable that the fence is removable as it is not always appropriate for the babies to be outside and a permanent barrier reduces the play possibilities for other children. Low canvas walls attached to verandah uprights have been found to be successful.

There are many tabletop activities that can be presented outside under a verandah; for example, construction toys, cushions and books, or a dramatic play area with props and furniture. Woodwork is an activity that needs to be done outside and under a verandah can be ideal, depending on the amount of reverberation into the building from vigorous hammering. If the noise is too disruptive the woodwork table is best under a canopy outside a nearby storage shed.

Schools often use the verandah as a place for children to have recess and lunch. Unfortunately the seating tends to be all along the wall with no opportunity for children to gain eye contact with friends while they are having their lunch. Socialising is extremely important, especially to the school-age children. Students have been known to sit on the cement floor in front of the seats so that they can talk to their friends. They need to have seats that face one another. A special lunch place with fixed tables and chairs in clusters, or movable furniture, would allow students to 'pull up a chair' and join their friends.

Ramp access is necessary in all early childhood settings. Apart from providing access for pushers, people in wheelchairs must be considered.

Seating

There are many types of seats suitable for playgrounds. They can be long tree trunks, tree stumps (timber rounds), flat rocks, flat timber fixed on top of low walls, bench seats and seats with backs. In fact, in a play situation children will sit anywhere where there is a flat surface. Seats have many purposes. It is important to know how seats are likely to be used before deciding on the type of seat to install.

SPECTATOR SEATS

These seats are usually found around ovals and sporting areas so the children can watch a game or their friends as they play. They are also useful for children when changing shoes or as a place to leave clothing while they play. Most spectator seats are bench seats, some have backs but most are simple planks of wood on uprights. They need to be the appropriate height for the users.

Bench seats can be placed on the edge of paths and are useful either side of swing areas for children to use while waiting for a turn or while talking to friends who are swinging. Bench seats placed either side of swing areas can act as a barrier to children unthinkingly running into a moving swing. If several bench seats are placed so that children can have eye contact with others, then they will be used by groups of children as a meeting place.

Seats around trees are a variation of a spectator seat as all who sit on them face outwards. These are not useful unless there is something to see from all sides. A seat around a tree near a fence means that the outlook towards the fence is anything but interesting. Space should be allowed between the tree and the seat to prevent the tree being ring-barked as it grows. In these situations it is better to make the seating in a semi-circle so that it provides a good watching place.

SEATS FOR SOCIALISING

These types of seats are important for all ages because early childhood staff are continually encouraging and supporting children in developing social skills. It is most important for children to learn to interact with others appropriately. Most early childhood playgrounds do not have enough seats in the play area for children to use. They should be presented in a variety of ways and forms. A cubbyhouse needs seats. Bush cubbies lend themselves to tree logs or tree-trunk seats while flat smooth rocks placed in a digging area or at the side of a sandpit can be used as either seats or tables.

Most early childhood centres and schools have a policy of 'no hat, no play' and all the children are supposed to have sunscreen on before they go outside. Sunscreen does protect the children to a certain extent but not completely (see Appendix 4). All centres should have a policy regarding the application of sunscreen.

Seating must also be provided in gazebos, and on verandahs. The arrangement of the seating will depend on whether the purpose of the seating is for socialising or for spectator use. If the seats are for socialising, they must face one another.

Shade

> Direct ultraviolet rays are distributed by the sun's beam. Indirect ultraviolet rays are scattered and reflected by many different materials in the environment. These include particles in the atmosphere and water droplets in clouds, as well as a variety of surfaces such as water, sand and concrete.
>
> (Department of Architecture, University of Queensland, 1997, p. 8)

Small shade structures do not provide enough protection from the ultraviolet rays as radiation and reflection from nearby cement or light-coloured buildings will reach under the structure. Make sure that the size of the shade structure is much larger than the area it is supposed to be shading. If it is not large enough, canopies can be attached to the sides to enlarge the shaded area.

A structure that is shaded in the morning is not necessarily shaded in the afternoon. If children are going to be using such an area in the afternoon then it must have the shaded area enlarged or have movable shade structures attached.

The planting of densely foliaged trees will protect an area from ultraviolet rays but it takes time for trees to grow. Temporary shelters can be erected until the trees grow to ensure that the children are protected. Also, grass does not reflect ultraviolet rays as much as hard surfaces.

All areas where children spend long uninterrupted periods of time must be well shaded; areas such as sandpits, climbing equipment, construction and dramatic play areas, amphitheatres and seating.

Fixed play equipment

The main purpose of fixed play equipment is to provide opportunities for children to engage in gross motor activities, such as swinging, climbing, crawling, hanging, sliding and balancing. All fixed play equipment must have impact-absorbing surfaces underneath and around the structure (see information on Australian Standards at the beginning of this chapter, p. 1).

It is a grave mistake to install one piece of this type of equipment and expect it to be suitable for all ages, or for it to cater to all the children's needs. This equipment must be age-appropriate. Because of the cost of fixed play equipment many preschool and school playgrounds have only the one piece of fixed climbing equipment. For very young children this could be dangerous as the structures are too high and the handrails do not suit the age group.

Older children tend to create challenges for themselves by using the climbing equipment inappropriately, such as climbing along the top, walking along the outside of the safety rails or sliding down the outside of a tunnel slide. Naylor (1985, p.125) points out:

> ... from informal observations, a structurally sound piece of equipment can still give rise to accidents not envisaged by the designer. Children run up slides ... Similarly on swings once children get bored with the normal method of swinging, they may try kneeling on the swing, shortening the swing chains or even climbing on the frame ...

Swings

Swings appeal to a wide age-range of children and researchers (Naylor 1985; Senda 1992) attribute the appeal to feelings of dizziness due to the speed and height. Fox and Dempsey (in their 1996 study, p. 43) found the benefits of swinging activities covered all areas of children's development and have listed the various stages of children's swinging behaviours. Many parts of the body are used during swinging as children use their legs to pump the swing up and they move their upper body backwards and forwards to maintain rhythm. It requires considerable balance and coordination of the whole body to achieve success as a 'swinger'.

When researching the use of swings by children three to five years, Berry (1993, p. 119) found that girls had less difficulty learning to swing than boys. Boys held their bodies and arms rigid and tended to rock backwards and forwards, whereas the girls seemed to have a natural rhythm. However, with more practice and staff encouragement the boys' swinging skills gradually improved. The Australian Health and Fitness Survey 1985, in a test to measure flexibility in children 7–15 years, also found that girls were more flexible in the lower back and hamstrings than boys at all ages.

● Grant (four years, seven months) lay across the seat of the swing with his arms and legs dangling either side. He pushed his feet on the ground and managed to move the swing backwards and forwards for a few minutes. He then turned the swing around and around until the ropes were twisted tight with him inside. He then lifted his feet off the ground allowing the swing to whiz around and around.

'We don't do whizzies on swings Grant!', said the teacher. 'Swings have seats that are there to sit on. Sit on the swing and swing properly!' ●

How often have we heard this comment? We now know from the research that boys need help, as they find it easier to have whizzies than try to work the swing up high.

A double swing frame allows children to socialise with their peers, talking as they swing, particularly if both swing attachments are similar. Experienced swingers will often encourage a friend to practise swinging or even give instructions on how to pump up the swing. Girls in particular are very competitive on the swings and attaching a basket-tyre swing next to a tyre-strap swing sets up a situation for a winner and a loser. A basket-tyre swing is not as easy to swing up high. Bench seats at the side of swing frame areas also allow other children to join in the discussions as they wait for a turn on the swings.

During Berry's observations of children's use of swings a child was seen standing next to an empty basket-tyre swing for 20 minutes waiting for a turn while her friend used the strap-swing . Once the friend had left the strap-swing the girl sat on the strap-swing and began to swing.

Swing frames, for all ages other than for the babies, need to be double frames with pigtail hooks to allow for different swing attachments when appropriate. It also protects the swing attachments in areas of high vandalism as the swings can be removed when not in use. Never have a third attachment in between the two swings as a child could be caught in the middle or get knocked by a moving swing when trying to leave the area.

In preschools, swing frames need to be placed where the swingers can see the whole of the playground while swinging. Preschoolers use swings as a watching place, often moving on to another activity from the swings after observing the activity from a 'safe' distance. Ideally all swing frames should not face full sun, as children cannot see with the sun in their eyes.

It is also important that the swing-area is positioned in a corner or where at least the back of the swing-area is next to a fence. This reduces the possibility of children running into the back of a swing. A garden bed on one or both sides with a narrow access path into the area would reduce the possibility of children running into a moving swing. Aesthetically gardens are preferable to low fencing as fencing gives a 'caged animal' impression. Bench seats on the sides of a swing area will also act as a barrier as children will slow down when they see a seat.

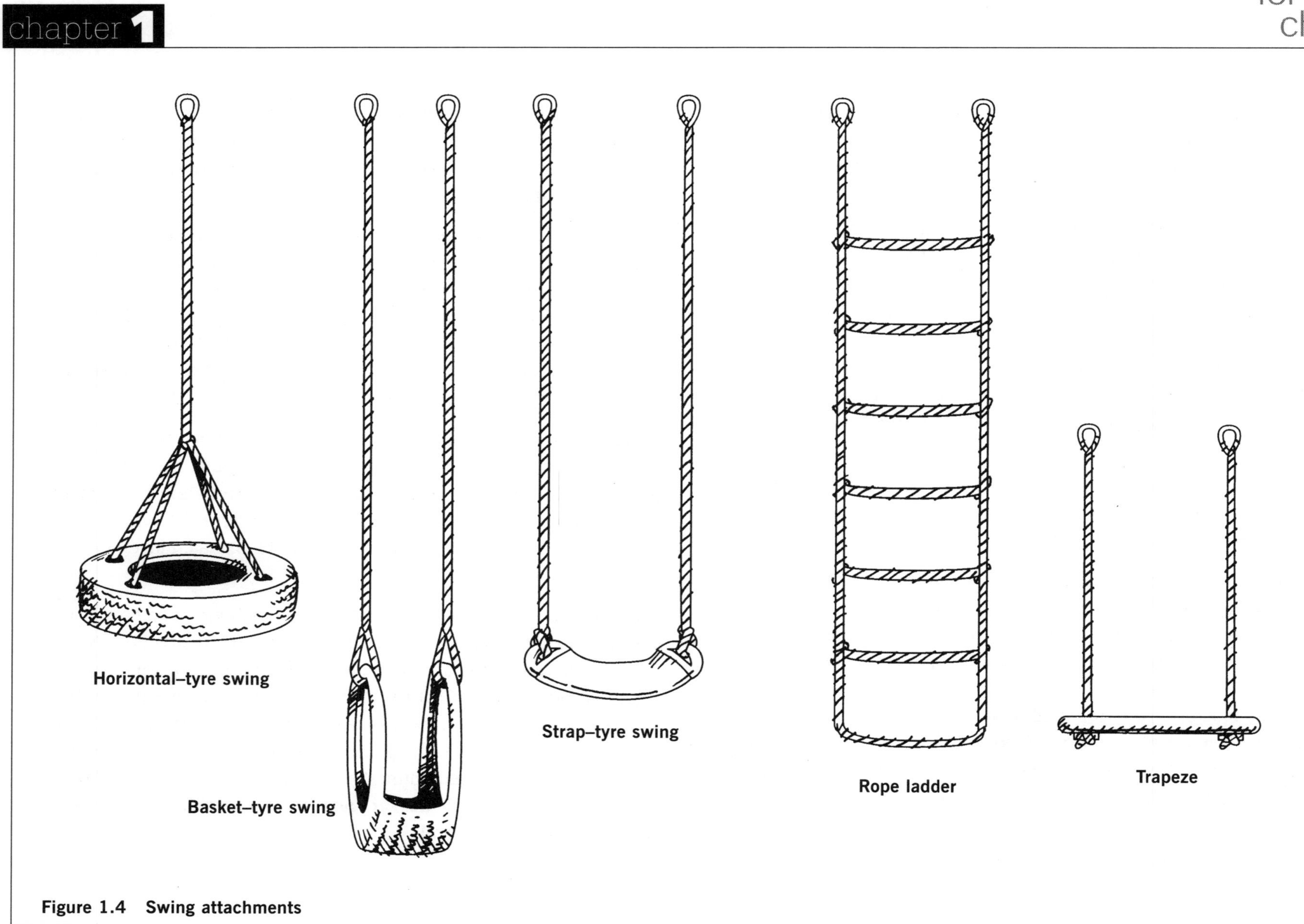

Figure 1.4 Swing attachments

SWING ATTACHMENTS

Various swing attachments are shown in Figure 1.4.

Baby swing

This must have a high back and sides to support the baby's back with a front fastener or a divided space for the legs to fit through for safety. It needs to have a short rope so that the swinging arc is small and the seat low to the ground. It is important for the carer to be present at all times while the baby is in the swing, and the caregiver must be sure to move the swing gently.

Some swings are placed at an adult's eye-level so that the carer and the baby have eye contact at all times and can interact with one another. However, extra special care must be taken if this practice is to be adopted and appropriate impact-absorbing surfaces must be provided.

Basket-tyre swing

This swing still gives the child support at the back and sides to hang onto. It is suitable for a beginning swinger and for children who are nervous or insecure and need an adult to push the swing for them. A child feels secure in this type of swing.

Strap-tyre swing

This is the swing for the serious 'swinger' as the child has freedom from side restraints and is able to pump the swing up high. It is always best if there are two of these swings side by side as it allows friends, at a similar stage of development as a swinger, the opportunity to talk as they swing.

Horizontal-tyre-swing

This attachment needs a lot of space. It should be the only attachment on the double swing frame due to the pivotal swinging in all directions. It is ideal for promoting co-operation between children as two children can sit on it and swing, but only if they can coordinate their movements.

Trapeze

This attachment is more suitable for junior primary children as preschoolers do not have the strength in their arms to maintain a grip for long. They often finish sitting on the bar using it as a swing without much success. Some of these trapeze attachments have loops hanging down each side of the bar, and these seem easier for the younger children. This attachment is good for upper body development.

Tarzan rope or knotted foot loop

These are more suited to the junior primary children. It is important to ensure that children on these attachments do no crash into the uprights of the frame.

Rope ladders

These are suitable for junior primary children. They are very difficult for preschool children as the ladder cannot be fastened at the base due to safety requirements. Metal pegs placed in the ground to anchor the ladder present a safety hazard as children may fall onto them. Preschoolers step onto the first rung successfully but when they step onto the next rung the ladder swings out in front of them, their bottoms drop down and they are unable to climb any higher. Knotted foot loop attachments are also best suited to the older child.

Staff need to be prepared to change the swing attachments according to the needs and stage of development of the children.

Placing one strap swing and one basket swing on a frame, which has been the usual practice by early childhood staff, is appropriate if the children wanting a swing have different needs.

Swings are an area where preschool girls tend to dominate (see Table 1.1). It is important to make sure that boys get a chance and are encouraged and supported when using the swings so that they can develop coordination and balance skills.

It is most important that impact-absorbing materials are placed in all swing areas. There are definite guidelines on the depth and area of soft-fall materials and the types of materials that are most suitable. Check the Australian Standards for details.

Frost (1992, p. 220) reports that the most common accidents with swings in America are:

- a child falling from a swing onto a hard surface
- a child falling from a swing and being hit on the head by the swing seat
- a child walking into the path of a moving swing.

These findings are also applicable in Australia. However, most of these accidents can be overcome by making sure that there is an appropriate impact-absorbing surface under the swing, that the swing seat is made of soft rubber, and the swing is positioned where a child is less likely to walk into a moving swing.

Make sure there are no entrapment hazards, particularly with the baby swings. Check the Australian Standards for details.

TABLE 1.1 CHILDREN'S USE OF SWINGS

Centre A	all children	girls	boys
Number of children	20	15	5
Average time (minutes)	5.35	6.8	1
Centre B	**all children**	**girls**	**boys**
Number of children	24	21	3
Average time (minutes)	3.1	3.3	2
Centre D	**all children**	**girls**	**boys**
Number of children	16	12	4
Average time (minutes)	3.37	3.75	2.2

Note: These figures were recorded from six observations of 20 minutes duration with no adult interactions with the children.

Source: Berry, P. (1993) Young Children's Use of Fixed Playground Equipment. In *International Play Journal* Vol 1 No 2, May pp. 115–31, Chapman & Hall, London.

Slides

Slides are very popular with all children. They offer children the opportunity to experience the feelings of speed and height. Children will experiment with different ways of going down the slide, feet first, head first, and sometimes sideways. They will roll objects down a slide and much to the displeasure of staff they will walk up a slide causing traffic jams at the top, or a collision halfway down.

There are a variety of slides available — straight, curvy, wide and tunnel slides. Steele and Nauman (1985, pp. 121–7) found that in a group of children aged four months to three years, a tunnel slide was used more by the older children than the younger ones. Berry (1993) observed that in a child-care centre playground where there was no quiet place for the children to go, they used the tunnel slide as a secret place. This proved to be a dangerous practice as older children often came hurtling down on top of them, resulting in minor injuries. Tunnel slides are not recommended for toddlers.

Slides are best positioned in a mound, if the playground is large enough to accommodate a mound. If not, the slide needs to be attached to another piece of play equipment (see the section on mounds later in this chapter). Slides need to act like a pathway, when children slide down to the bottom, they need to see something of interest in front of them to encourage them to explore another play option when they have finished sliding. Slides that leave children facing a fence on completion of their slide restrict the children's play options. The height of the slides must be appropriate to the age of the users.

A mounded slide or one attached to play equipment is preferable to a self-standing slide as it reduces the possible fall height. Slides with a slow finish are more suited to children in the early childhood years as their bodies are almost at a stop by the time they reach the ground. This also reduces the amount of hollowing out at the bottom and prevents the children from becoming projectiles as they shoot off the end of the slide. There is also the danger of back injuries if children shoot off the end of the slide and land on their bottoms. The placing of sand at the bottom of a slide to absorb any impact can also present a safety hazard. Unless it is covered with rubber matting, young children will see the sand as a place to play and they could get hurt by another child sliding down on top of them.

Metal slides can become extremely hot in summer and can burn those who slide on them, whereas plastic slides do not retain as much heat as the metal ones. It is important that slides face south or as close as possible to south in the Southern Hemisphere and north in the Northern Hemisphere, to reduce the amount of sun on them during the day.

Climbing frames

Research has shown that climbing frames have little appeal to children. Noren-Bjorn (1982) found equipment for climbing only was used infrequently and at the most for about two minutes. Berry (1993) found climbing frames were only used when loose parts, such as dramatic play props or movable boards and ladders, were added.

School-age children use climbing frames mainly to sit on top and watch others at play. They are often used as a meeting place where groups of friends gather to talk. Young children tend to use the loose soft-fall material underneath the frame more than the actual frame itself.

Metal climbing frames become extremely hot in the sun and can burn children's hands and feet.

One centre draped old curtains or a canvas beach shelter over the top of the frame and used the area for a fire station, a hospital, and a cubby on various occasions, all furnished with the appropriate furniture and adjuncts.

Scramble nets

These need to be on a fixed frame for safety reasons. They must be firmly laced to a frame so that there is no possibility of the net slipping. (See Australian Standards for appropriate height.)

Scramble nets on a stand-alone frame do not hold children's interest. Once a child has climbed up and down there is nowhere else to go and they leave. If the frame is placed just above ground level on the side of a mound following the contour of the slope, it can be used as another way up the side of the slope. If it is part of a piece of fixed equipment, it is usually as a way up or down from the structure. Make sure that there is the appropriate depth of soft-fall underneath.

Turn-over bars

Turn-over bars provide children over five years of age with the opportunity to lift their own weight, which helps with the development of the upper body. They hang by their legs or arms and do a variety of tricks, often to impress friends or adults who may be watching.

Children under five use the turn-over bars fleetingly as they do not have the strength to support their whole body weight. Turn-over bars are more suited to junior primary aged children.

Two parallel turn-over bars with enough space between them to fit a child in a wheelchair will provide upper body exercise for children in wheelchairs.

Berry (1993) found that children under five years used turn-over bars mainly as a meeting place, something to lean on when talking to friends. One five-year-old girl, however, used the turn-over bars for an average of six minutes in four 20-minute observations (see Appendix 1).

Horizontal ladders, hanging rings/triangles

These pieces of equipment provide for children's upper body development and require strength and agility to move from one end of the ladder to the other. Children over five will use them with friends in a competitive way or to show off their skills.

Berry found children nearing five years of age used the horizontal ladder in between other activities; when they had finished playing in the sandpit, or when waiting for a friend to come outside to play. They also spent time on top of the structure watching other children at play.

The length of time spent on horizontal ladders was very short, averaging approximately two minutes. When staff stayed in the area and interacted with the children the time spent doubled (see Appendix 1).

In one centre, climbing on top of the horizontal ladder at 'packing-up' time it was a popular pastime — obviously with the hope of escaping the packing-up work. It is not appropriate for children to climb onto the top of horizontal ladders as falls through the bars to the ground can result in broken bones. Injury records support this fact.

Balance beams

Children will walk along balancing on edges of garden beds, house foundations, rocks and tree stumps on the way to another area or as part of a made-up game, but will seldom spend time on manufactured balance beams unless they are part of a supervised circuit in a school yard.

Balancing activities need to be made more interesting, and challenging. Stepping stone paths leading to places of interest, or wide low tree stumps placed a child's-step away from one another have more appeal than the manufactured beams.

Clatterbridges

Clatterbridges are not really suitable for very young children who are uncertain on their feet. They need to master walking and climbing on the ground before tackling ground that moves, however they are a lot of fun for five- to eight-year-old children. Regular maintenance is needed to tighten the chains and to check that the spaces between the slats do not trap the children's feet as they run across the bridge.

Older children test their ability to walk or run on the bridge without losing their balance and falling over. However, unless the bridge leads to somewhere of interest, it is of limited value. One centre built a sandpit next to an existing clatterbridge and placed a creek feeding water under the bridge into the sandpit. This did increase the use as children used it as a watching place and somewhere to go fishing. Other centres and schools have used low clatterbridges to link two mounds and created a dry creek bed as an area for children to use in their dramatic play.

Fixed bridges

Small bridges can draw children into an area that is often overlooked. They can be placed on a narrow path leading to a bush cubby or over a watercourse. They can be used to encourage children to use a certain path instead of cutting corners.

In one centre the access path to the building was around a square lawn. Children were continually cutting the corner of the lawn to enter the building as it was the most direct path. To overcome this habit a small bridge was placed on a narrow soft-surface path in a direct line from the front gate to the front door of the building. Bushy shrubs were planted either side of the bridge to give a cosy effect. Children began to use the bridge when they arrived and also used the area for their dramatic play during session time.

Another centre had a long straight cement path from the front gate to the front door of the building. Children would run down the path on arrival and invariably fall over and arrive crying and needing a band-aid. A grandfather jokingly suggested that they place a speed hump in the path. After some discussion a small bridge suitable for pushers and wheelchairs was installed halfway along the path and this slowed the child traffic down on arrival.

Combined structures

These structures usually comprise a variety of components designed to cater mainly for children's physical needs. The age of the users should determine the type of components included in the structure. The components introduced previously in this section on fixed play equipment would all be suitable as part of a combined structure as they would add variety and interest to the children's play.

Gabbard (1979) (reported in Frost 1992) tested the effects of specific play apparatus experiences on four- to six-year-old children's upper body muscular endurance. Gabbard found that the provision of a variety of upper body movement experiences contributed to increased muscular endurance performance.

Combined structures are ideal for short-term play especially in community parks and playgrounds where caregivers and children visit occasionally and for a relatively short time, so the novelty value remains. They are usually brightly coloured and therefore attract the passer-by to the playground. They are also useful in school settings for short-term play at recess and lunchtime. If the components are carefully chosen to meet specific needs, they can become part of an exercise circuit of a physical education program.

In an early childhood centre where children are present for five days a week for up to four or five years they soon tire of these structures. Most of them cannot be added to and for those that can be changed, it is a major operation for busy staff. Children cannot make the changes as safety is a real issue in these situations.

The linking platforms are usually small and are used as a thoroughfare to all the play features as well as by children engaging in roving dramatic play. Any dramatic play components such as steering wheels cater for short-term dramatic play as children often use these structures as a base for their dramatic play themes.

Research on young children's use of fixed play equipment (Berry 1993) found that most combined structures did not provide staff or children with the opportunity to add to the structure. The space provided for dramatic play was only suitable for one or two children and the position of the dramatic play elements were in the way of children moving through to other sections and therefore destroyed the possibility of any sustained play.

Children in the zero to five age group did not use the abacus or the noughts and crosses and, contrary to some manufacturers' claims,

TABLE 1.2 CHILDREN'S USE OF COMBINED STRUCTURES

		STAGE 1			STAGE 2		
		all children	girls	boys	all children	girls	boys
Centre E	Number of children	34	23	11	42	22	20
	Average time (minutes)	5.5	6.1	4.1	4	2.9	5.3
Centre F	Number of children	42	32	10	51	31	21
	Average time (minutes)	3.1	3.3	2.5	8.3	8	8.7
Centre G	Number of children	51	26	25	59	39	20
	Average time (minutes)	5.9	6.5	5.36	10	11.5	7.2

Note: These figures were recorded from six observations of 20 minutes duration in Stage 1 with no adult interaction and no props or loose parts and six in Stage 2 with adult interaction with props and loose parts available.

the primary colours did not necessarily mean that children learnt their colours. So, are these extras necessary?

One combined structure (see Table 1.2 Centre E) had a small platform with a porthole and a steering wheel on one side, a vertical corkscrew climb with a fire-fighters' pole was next to it, and a horizontal open ring/tunnel on the other side that led to the tunnel slide attached to the small platform. Dramatic play was continually disturbed by children using the slide, tunnel and corkscrew climb.

Another combined structure (see Table 1.2 Centre F) had a very small cubby area in the middle where children continually ran past to get to the slide on a platform at the end of the structure.

Underneath the cubby section was a shopfront that was seldom used as a shop, but often the counter was used for climbing. Unless staff set up the shop front with the children as a shop, it had very little relevance. On the other end were two large platforms suitable for furniture and props, however, the staff never placed anything on those platforms so they were a waste of space. During Stage 2 of the research project on Children's Use of Fixed Equipment (see Appendix 1 and Table 1.2) staff were asked to add furniture and dress-ups to the platforms and this resulted in children spending longer in the area.

The platforms had been positioned so that the children could enter and leave those particular platforms without traversing the whole structure and, while the play elements were appropriate, it would have been preferable if the platforms promoting the dramatic play had been furnished as part of the normal program.

Dramatic play structures

> Most children around the world between the ages of two and eight engage in a form of voluntary social play activity we refer to as dramatic or socio-dramatic play.
>
> (Smilansky 1990, p. 18)

Studies by Smilansky and others have found that this kind of play is a strong medium for the development of socio-emotional and cognitive skills. It is important therefore that provisions are made in the outdoors for this type of play. Children need a variety of areas where dramatic play can be nurtured. It will depend on the age and stage of the children what is most appropriate. For the very young a table, chair and a telephone or some plastic cups and plates — familiar objects — placed on the verandah, will enable the children to act out the roles of different members of their family.

> Socio-dramatic play peaks in children between the ages of four and six years.
>
> (Creaser 1990a, p. 8)

Children between four and five years tend to engage in socio-dramatic play with groups of approximately five but sometimes up to eight children. When most of the children are engaged in dramatic play at the same time, there is often not enough places suitable for them to make their bases. It is, therefore, important when developing a playground that a variety of options are considered. They do not all need to be constructions, some of them can be open spaces suitable for large block construction, places to pitch a tent, or a bush cubby made under a weeping tree or several bushy shrubs.

Children six and over do not need as many props or furniture in their dramatic and fantasy play as their imagination and language supply most of their needs, as is shown in the comment below:

> Let's pretend I am Hercules and we are looking for baby monsters in that long grass over there.

Cubbyhouses

Cubbyhouses are ideal for children under three as they enjoy sitting inside. They also like to take sand into a cubby and pour it over the floor — they can be encouraged to sweep it out again. The cubby needs to have two ways of entering and exiting as most children under two do not enjoy enclosed spaces. It needs to be close to the ground with a low ramp access so that they can take push–pull toys inside. A small amount of furniture needs to be in the cubby, just enough for one or two children as children at this age generally play alone or parallel to another child.

Figure 1.5 An open cubby for toddlers

When children's social skills develop, they like to play in a group. A cubbyhouse usually does not have enough room for a group of children and furniture, especially if it is to have two ways of entering and exiting. The more children using the cubby the less furniture that will fit inside.

A cubbyhouse without furniture and props is either not used, or is used inappropriately:

- A small cubbyhouse on stilts with ramps and a narrow platform in the front had stood in the playground for many years taking up a large area. Older brothers and sisters could remember it and spoke fondly of it. When children's use of the cubby was recorded it was found that children used the ramps and the platform out the front when playing chasings but seldom used the cubbyhouse. It was small with one open window and a doorway, so there was very little room for furniture and, because it was up on stilts, staff rarely put prop boxes inside. Children used it mainly to climb in and out of the window, or to trap someone inside by barricading the doorway. ●

If a centre has a cubbyhouse that is not being used very often, or it becomes very crowded affecting the quality of play, lower it and pave out the front then place bench seats on two sides to provide a place for an extension of play from the cubby. Do not put seats all the way around the paved area as this will affect the child traffic flow to and from the area.

Another option is to place a picnic table and bench seats to one side of the paved area and place suitable props in the area to extend the play. For example, if there are dolls beds and dolls in the cubbyhouse, prams or babies baths could be placed outside to be used as an extension of the play inside. (See Appendix 3. Centre D used the lawn area directly in front of their cubby for props and furniture to extend the play.) Figure 1.5 shows toddlers with push–pull toys in an open cubby.

Figure 1.6 Play platform

Play platforms/stages

Children need large platform areas that can be set up in a variety of ways. A large platform will allow room for children over two years to construct with building blocks or construction toys. Furniture and props can be placed on the platform to create a hospital, an office, a ship or truck depending on the interest of the children. Cushions and books or musical instruments can be placed in the area to give children a special place to read or experiment with simple instruments exploring sounds.

The platform needs to be large enough for up to five children plus furniture and props, and low enough not to present a safety hazard. It is important that the platform is not a thoroughfare to another play feature as child traffic will disturb the pretend play. For pretend play to develop and be sustained children need uninterrupted time and space.

Some play platforms consist of several platforms joined together. It is useful to have more than one section. All platforms need to be kept low — nothing over 800 mm for safety reasons unless a slide is to be included. A small platform suitable for a slide can be attached to the structure but it is better if access is not through the main platform, but by separate steps.

In a two-sectioned platform, one section can be designed to have galvanised piping between upright posts at a height of approximately 500 mm and 800 mm off the ground where movable boards, ladders and slide boards can be attached when appropriate (see Figure 1.6). This will encourage children to climb, balance and slide as part of entering the dramatic play.

If movable boards and ladders are to be attached to the platform it is best if the platform has impact-absorbing material around the climbing area, at the recommended depth (refer to Australian Standards titles on p. 1).

The other section can be used for the furniture, props or construction toys. It will need a separate entry and exit point to allow for the play to continue undisturbed by vigorous physical play activity on the climbing section. However, there must also be access to and from the lower platform. A very low platform with ramp access would provide for wheelchairs and push–pull toys.

These platforms are only successful if staff are prepared to provide props and furniture to support the children's play. (See Appendix 3 for length of time children of four to five years old spent in platforms that had furniture and props provided.)

It is important that platforms have generous shade placed over them or attached to them to ensure children will have protection from the sun. This is an area where children will play for long periods of time and they will need protection. The area needs to feel private and cosy so it will need fencing around the sides to give it an enclosed feel. These platforms are best positioned reasonably close to a storage area so that staff and children can access the props and furniture. Play platforms out of sight of the main play area are seldom used by children under five years old.

Information on poisonous plants, or where to find that information can be obtained from the botanical gardens in your capital city.

School-age children will still engage in pretend and fantasy play as well as acting out plays they have seen or written. A stage made of decking similar to the play platform will provide an area specifically for this kind of activity. The main difference is that the stage will need entry points either side and long steps across the front where children can make grand entrances and exits, or just use the steps as seats at recess or lunchtime.

The stage will need to be enclosed on three sides to provide an area where students feel protected. If the stage is placed in an area where there is space in front, it could be used for performances in fine weather.

It is useful for boxes of props to be made available to the children so that they can set up their own dramatic play situation. Some centres have a section in the storage shed where children can go and help themselves to certain props to support their play. In schools children can be made responsible for the collection and return of the props.

Jetties/wharves

Some centres or schools are situated close to the beach or a river and the children's interests and knowledge of water activities is greater than those of children living inland. In these situations it could be useful to construct a jetty or wharf where children can go 'fishing'.

Jetties need to be constructed so that they conform to the Australian Standards. They need to have fencing either side, steps up, handrails, and soft-fall underneath and look like jetties. The best jetties are no higher than 500 mm. An outline of a boat approximately 300 mm high made of timber next to the jetty will extend the play as the children can climb up and down into the boat as part of their pretend play.

Boats

Research has found that children do very little in a boat. At most, all they do is sit in it or climb over it. However, if the boat is positioned next to a jetty or wharf, it will be used as an extension of the jetty play.

An outline of a boat can be constructed next to the jetty or wharf to be used as an extension to the fishing themes. Some centres are given an old boat for the children to use. It is not ideal to use structures that are not built specifically for children's play as they tend to have sharp edges, or corners where spiders lurk. A replica of a boat without the safety hazards is preferable. Sand or seaweed placed on the ground around the boat and jetty make the area more realistic. However, if movable climbing boards and ladders are to be attached to the structures, soft-fall at the recommended depth is essential.

Natural play features

Landscaping for play

> Natural features are also important qualities of playgrounds ... the prevailing practice of considering such features to be secondary in importance to manufactured ones is a grievous error ... Natural features allow a wide range of learning opportunities not available from other playground options.
>
> (Frost 1992, p. 103)

PLANTING FOR PLAY

Plants not only make a playground more attractive to look at, if carefully chosen they will also offer a variety of features that will enrich the play experiences of all who use the area. It is important to consider the characteristics of the plants so that they can be chosen and positioned for a specific purpose. It may be for shade; to create a cosy environment; to provide a bushy place for a bush cubby; to attract native birds, butterflies and other insects; to add colour and textures; to show the change of seasons; to provide protection from the wind and privacy from passers-by; or to provide an extension to the curriculum.

Plant trees and shrubs of different textures, colours and perfumes; leaves with smooth edges and some with serrated edges; shiny leaves and others rough; trees and shrubs that lose their leaves and have beautiful autumn colours as well as others that are evergreen.

It is important to choose hardy inexpensive plants so that they can be replaced if damaged. Remember a playground is firstly a place for children, where everything in the area is dedicated to enriching play. Secondly it needs to be attractive so that children will enjoy playing in the area. A beautiful garden where children can only look and not touch has no place in an early childhood playground. If children are to learn about the world around them they need to have a sense of ownership and feel free to explore and discover the wonders of nature. At the same time children need to learn with the help of the adults around them to respect their environment.

Specific information on suitable plants has not been included in this book as the suitability of plants varies greatly from state to state and region to region. Centres need to contact their local plant nurseries or a horticulturalist for advice on appropriate planting for their particular area.

CHILDREN'S GARDENS

Children are extremely interested in plants and planting. However, it is important that all planting is carried out by the children with help and encouragement from staff. Children who are involved in the whole process will gain some ownership and are more likely to maintain an interest throughout the life of the plants. Quick-growing plants are best for the very young as they do not have the ability to delay gratification.

Long narrow garden beds with paths every metre are a good idea. Make them approximately a metre wide, to allow children to work in the area without treading on other plants. Place a tap nearby and attach a simple watering system to ensure the plants survive.

Encourage the children to water the plants and provide small watering cans so that they can water their plants and observe the growth whenever they show interest. Position the garden on the side of the play area so that the children do not feel the need to run through it on the way to other play features.

Vegetables and herbs can be used in cooking activities and flowers can be picked for use in play, for decorations, or for pressing to be used later. Vegetables can be planted to feed the rabbits or guinea pigs.

Schools can use planting and plants as part of their curriculum in mathematics, science, technology, society and the environment. Some schools have garden beds for each class where, depending on the age of the children, they learn about fruits, herbs and vegetables. These experiences are then extended to include information about native foods, foods of other cultures, crops, pest control, natural fertilisers, and composting.

Raised garden beds give children in wheelchairs the opportunity to become involved in the planting and maintenance of gardens.

SENSORY GARDENS

These gardens are best provided either side of narrow, winding, exploratory paths where children walk single file through plants of different perfumes, textures, colours.

It is important that these paths lead somewhere otherwise children will not walk through. A garden seat at the end of the path, a sundial, or a gazebo will provide a reason for children to use the path.

The narrowness of the path results in the plants brushing against the children as they walk so that the perfume of the plant is released. Archways with climbing perfumed plants hanging down to brush against the children also enhance the experience and encourage children to enter the sensory garden.

SECRET PLACES AND BUSH CUBBIES

Plant groups of shrubs with soft bushy foliage that will provide children with a quiet place to sit or play with a few friends. It is important, especially in child-care centres where children spend long days with a large group of children, that they have somewhere to withdraw from the noise and boisterous activities — where they can create a special place to take toys for quiet play.

Small trees that have drooping branches will also provide a special place or bush cubby that can be set up with furniture and props, such as dress-ups, for dramatic play.

MOUNDS

It depends on the available space whether a mound is a worthwhile proposition for an early childhood playground. Child-care centres and stand-alone preschools do not usually have sufficient room to create a mound of any significance.

Many centres have had small steep mounds placed in the playground at great cost with a slide installed into the slope. Most of these mounds become eroded in a short time and have been very difficult to repair. When the gradient exceeds one in three it is extremely difficult to keep grass growing on the slope and the erosion from wind, rain and children's feet turns the mound into a dangerous mud slide.

Mounds need to be long and low with gently sloping sides to overcome the erosion problem. They need to be positioned on the side or back of the play area so that they do not cut a playground in half. A mound can be a very big obstacle to young children and it can deter children from using play areas that are obscured from their sight.

Mounds add interest and height to often uninteresting play environments. In a setting where there is plenty of room to create a mound, or in one that is already mounded or sloped, the area can be furnished with many of the experiences found in combined structures. Some ideas include steps of different types to climb up to the top of the mound, a slide set into the mound, a scramble net on a frame on the side of the mound, winding paths leading to a sanded area on top where toy cars or dolls can be used in pretend play or a sitting area on top where children can see the whole playground. Sensory plants can be planted either side of some of the paths and a 'fallen' tree trunk provides an interesting place to sit or play. A path can lead to a clatterbridge over an undulation. Make sure the clatterbridge has handrails suitable for the age group and that the bridge is not high off the ground so as to reduce the problem of falls from the bridge. A watercourse meandering down the mound or under the clatterbridge and around rocks could enter a sandpit at the base of the mound.

It is very important that the materials used in mound constructions do not contain rocks and hard rubbish that are larger than a tennis ball as these often work their way to the surface causing safety hazards. Any hard matter must be well buried in the centre of the base of any large mound and not used in the construction of any small mounds. Good quality topsoil must be placed on top of the mound so that grass or hardy ground covers can grow successfully. Mounds built of rubbish soil result in mountains of hard bare earth.

Small undulations rather than mounds of approximately 200 mm to 300 mm will provide a place for young babies to crawl and toddlers to climb and roll down and will add interest to an otherwise flat playground.

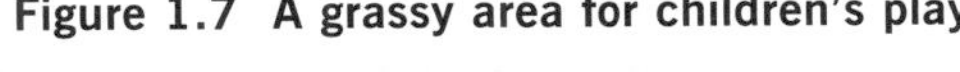

Figure 1.7 A grassy area for children's play

Ground surfaces

It is important to decide what type of play is likely to take place in each area of the playground before deciding on the ground surfacing.

SOFT SURFACING

Grass is a popular choice as it provides a place to spread a rug and introduce different activities according to the age and interests of the children. Very young children need a large area of soft surfaces, especially those who are still crawling or are unsure on their feet. Grass can be grown on a mound if the slope is gentle. Figure 1.7 shows children throwing bean bags into a framed net on the grass.

Flat grassy areas provide a soft base for constructing with outdoor wooden blocks, a place to pitch a tent or a place to play organised ball games and group games. Tables can be placed on the grass with tabletop toys, babies baths or finger painting activities. Grass surfacing makes it easier to clean up after messy tabletop activities.

Schools need grassed ovals to provide for the many sporting activities school-age children engage in. Long grass is fun for children to play in, as it promotes dramatic and socio-dramatic play. Children need large uncluttered areas of grass for running, throwing and kicking balls and rolling hoops.

Young children see sand as a place to play and for this reason sand should be avoided around and under play equipment. Older children could fall on top of younger children playing in the area.

Surfaces made of recycled rubber have been found to be suitable but not as effective as wood chips. However, there are situations where these products, although very expensive, are preferable; for example, under swings or in playgrounds for children under two where they are likely to put the wood chips in their mouths.

Check the Standards on surfacing before making a decision (refer to information on p. 1).

Matching the type of grass with where it is to be grown is extremely important. Some grass can be highly irritating for hay fever and asthma sufferers in the Spring. Grass does not survive the constant wear and tear of children's feet. Landscapers and lawn experts may underestimate the damage children's feet cause. Look at the playground and decide where the child traffic is likely to be heaviest and avoid using grass as the surface in those areas. Children take the shortest possible path to favourite activities, which means they cut corners and deviate from existing paths. Grass does not survive in heavily shaded areas. Choose a hard-wearing type of grass, plant it in sunny situations, and water well.

Garden mulch provides a soft surface. If it is deep enough it will provide a spongy surface for children to walk on. Sawdust is another material sometimes used for informal paths. Many of our botanical gardens use garden mulch or sawdust for paths. Ground-covering plants offer a soft surface but they are usually either too fine to cope with heavy wear and tear or too hardy and uneven under foot.

IMPACT-ABSORBING SURFACES

All playground equipment needs to have an impact-absorbing surface underneath and out from equipment (see the Australian Standards on Playground Surfacing (AS/NZS 4422:1996) for recommended area and depth). There is no perfect impact-absorbing surface, however some are much better than others.

Wood-chips have been found to be the most effective as far as impact absorbency is concerned, however they do need to be maintained at the required depth. Some other loose materials have been found to be equally effective under certain conditions, but they must be tested before use.

In Australia, grass is not an impact-absorbing material. Our long hot summers dry out the soil and it becomes like cement underneath. Sand is not always suitable; it depends on the type of sand, some sand acts like cement on impact. It is important that all sand is tested for its impact absorbency before installation.

HARD SURFACES

Young children need a smooth hard surface where they can use ride-on and push–pull toys. Staff in early childhood centres need hard surface areas where they can place tables and chairs for a variety of tabletop activities or set up furniture for dramatic play or construction. Children in schools need hard surfaces to play some ball games, such as handball, basketball and netball, and hard wall surfaces that children can hit or throw balls against.

Asphalt, cement and brick paving all provide a hard surface but they can also radiate a tremendous amount of heat in summer. Large areas of light coloured cement can create a problem with glare in summer and will reflect ultraviolet rays so it is important to keep the cement to a minimum or cover it in shade. (Refer to section on Shade earlier in this chapter.)

PATHWAYS

> A path is the empty space on the ground through which people move in getting from one place to another; it need be no different in composition from the rest of the surface.
>
> (Kritchevsky et al. 1977, p. 17)

The important task of paths is to lead to something of interest and make the journey there enjoyable. Sometimes a path leads under an archway or over a bridge, sometimes it can be flanked either side with perfumed plants. It can lead to a secret place, a sitting area, a sanded area for making roads, or provide a place to practise jumping.

When planning a playground, space must be left between fixed structures to act as a pathway so that children can move freely from one play feature to another. When setting up movable equipment children still need that space between the equipment. If space is limited the equipment will act as a barrier to other play features.

Informal paths designed to extend children's play opportunities can be made from a variety of surfaces. They can be of garden mulch, sawdust, compacted building sand, timber rounds, stepping stones or be just a space between play equipment. Narrow paths encourage children to walk single file and reduce running. If an exploratory path winds around and through trees and shrubs, with collections of pine cones, smooth river stones or some other natural materials for children to collect, it adds to the appeal. If there is an element of mystery about where it leads or what is around the corner it usually appeals to older children, whereas younger children need to see what is at the end of the path.

Circular paths around a playground for tricycles and push–pull toys tend to cut the playground in half and create a safety hazard. A child running from one section of the playground to another can collide with a child on a bike, as both children can be so absorbed in what they are doing that they do not notice the other child. It is preferable for these paths to be placed at the side of a playground or at the back so that children do not have to go through the track to an activity on the other side.

Access paths need to be of a hard surface so that children with physical disabilities, especially those in wheelchairs, can move from one section to another with ease. Unless the centre is specifically for physically disabled children it is important that these access paths do not cut the playground in half restricting the play area for other children in the centre. Hard surfaced paths also need to be provided for staff to wheel equipment such a water troughs, or children's tricycles from the storage shed. If using pavers they need to be non-slip, and concrete needs to be brushed to reduce the possibility of children or staff slipping on the path.

EDGES

It is most important that raised edges are kept to a minimum in any playground. Edges create a barrier to young children, and can influence the child traffic flow around the playground. Children do not cross over paths, raised boundaries or anything they subconsciously see as obstacles. What they see as an obstacle is often not obvious to the adult. We need to see the play area through the eyes of children. When they are sitting in the sandpit, large rocks around the edge could be a barrier, if they are running towards the swing area, a bench seat on the edge of a swing area is a barrier.

Raised edges create a trip hazard for small children as they unthinkingly run around the playground. Although they can climb over many of the edges they tend to use flat entrances and exits in preference to raised ones. However, they will climb over raised edges on occasions if there is something on the other side that attracts their attention.

Sometimes it is not possible to excavate in which case the raised area needs to be at the back or sides of a playground so that it does not divide the playground in half in the same manner as a hard surface path can.

Soft-fall areas need to be excavated to the required depth for soft-fall (stated in the Australian Standards) and retained with edging that is at ground level. Sandpits should be excavated with part of the edging at ground level to allow for sand to be swept back into the sandpit. Sandpits can be edged with a variety of materials, such as paver-paths, timber, logs, tree trunks, flat or rounded rocks and plants. The use of several types of materials creates a more interesting environment for children.

Rocks in the playground must not have sharp edges, they need to be well weathered.

All concrete and brick edging must be smooth and rounded, timber needs to be sanded to avoid splinters.

chapter 2 Special considerations

There are certain variables that influence the type of playground suitable for different communities. Each local community has its own specific characteristics that staff and committees must be aware of when planning programs for the children.

It could be that a large proportion of the children in the community live in high-rise apartments and need the opportunity to run, play ball games and engage in vigorous physical activities, or children from a different cultures, where the Australian way of life is foreign and they need some of their own culture inserted into the play environment. Are there a large number of Aboriginal or Torres Straight Islander people living in the area who bring their own special culture, skills and lifestyle to the program?

There could be mainly single parents or families where both parents work and have no family support nearby, or parents with very young children who share the playground with older children while attending playgroup sessions. These factors need to be considered when designing a playground as it is important to cater for the needs of all the children. Figure 2.1 shows Sam using a push–pull toy.

Children with disabilities

If the centre may have children with disabilities enrolled in the program or who are visiting the playground through the week, it is important to consider them when designing the playground.

If the program is designed mainly for children with disabilities, then special equipment must be chosen for those specific disabilities. Consultation with specialists and staff who work with these children on the their specific needs is vital before designing the playground.

However, there are general play features that can be included that will suit many children and many disabilities — ones that will develop independence and a feeling of self-worth. The more natural environments, and in particular the sensory experiences — which include trees with rustling leaves, shrubs, flowers, gently undulating terrain, grass, sand and water and wide variety of colours, perfumes and textures — appeal to all children and give them the opportunity to discover for themselves the wonders of the world around them.

Hard surfaced paths leading to major play features are required for children with physical disabilities such as those with crutches, those unsteady on their feet, or those in wheelchairs. Children with impaired vision will need hard and soft textures under foot, textures that make different sounds when walked on so that they can experience the variations, brightly coloured flowers, bold contrasting colours to see and, for safety reasons, they will need barriers placed around all movable equipment, such as swings.

Figure 2.1 A vigorous physical activity

Children with physical and intellectual disabilities will need an environment that encourages them to move around and explore a variety of experiences and activities, ones that will give them the opportunity to touch, see, smell, taste and hear. They will need the support of adults encouraging and helping them to play creatively and spontaneously and to develop positive relationships. All children in the early childhood ages of birth to eight years need these experiences.

Children from Indigenous Australian families

It is most important that playgrounds used by Indigenous Australian children are relevant to their interests, lifestyle and skills. Although their play is similar to non-Indigenous children there are some differences in child-rearing practices that influence their play behaviour and that need to be recognised:

> In Aboriginal society, risk-taking is considered an important learning process for the children.
>
> (Johns 1999, p. 62 in *Child's Play*)

Sometimes this risk-taking can create a dilemma for staff in early childhood centres when they see children climbing and balancing along the top of a piece of climbing equipment instead of using the steps. Most safety rules and regulations do not encourage risk-taking. Australian Aboriginal children also engage in physical play fighting. Most early childhood staff intervene when children begin to engage in physical play fighting.

The following scenarios show how two different centres planned environments to cater for the interests and lifestyles of their children:

- 1. An Aboriginal Child-care Centre in a rural coastal town was allocated money for a new centre to be built and the Aboriginal staff had the opportunity to be part of the decision-making about what kind of playground would best suit the needs of their children and their families.

  The staff were asked to discuss the interests and lifestyles of the children in their care.

  Most of the families were involved in fishing. Large family groups as well as individuals would go fishing, sometimes in a boat or from a jetty or wharf. The children from the extended families were included and would spend the time fishing and exploring the environment. They were familiar with all the types of fish, the different types of shells that could be found in certain areas, and weather and tide patterns. It was an important part of their life and their play reflected this knowledge and interest.

  To cater for the children's imaginative play, low decking in the form of a wharf and a jetty were constructed, with a 'boat' next to the jetty. Sand was placed around and under the structures and coastal shrubs planted to create bush cubbies. Much of the work was carried out at weekends by the fathers and uncles in the extended family and the children were able to see them working so it became a family affair. Pride and ownership of that playground was evident in the families involved.

2. A suburban preschool mainly for Aboriginal children had a huge mound with a fort on the top of the mound. The playground was so small that the children could see into the garden next door from the top of the fort and balls and toys seemed to end up next door. The fort became dilapidated and unsafe and the mound, which was too steep and too large for such a small space, began to cave in. The whole structure and mound was then removed.

   Apart from the usual playground features such as swings, sandpit and climbing experiences, a more natural environment was developed in the area. An exploratory area with sensory paths and native bushes and shrubs was planted. Clumps of bushes created bush cubbies and different collections of seed pods were placed under some of the shrubs for the children to discover. Great pains were taken to choose plants that were native to the area. A watercourse with smooth river stones meandered under a bridge into a digging area that had several medium-sized rocks that the children could sit on or dig around. Children could dig for worms, observe the roots of weeds, and discover creatures that tend to live under rocks. ●

Shared space centres

Many early childhood centres, particularly the smaller ones, have limited outdoor space and have only one playground that needs to cater for children whose ages range from a few months old to five years. In situations such as this it is advisable to have a minimum of fixed structures, and those need to be low to the ground.

Toddlers tend to be adventurous and will climb anything, especially high climbing structures designed for older children. It is very difficult to supervise toddlers in a playground designed for older children. Safety is of prime importance.

Movable climbing equipment, such as boards and ladders that can be attached to low fixed structures, and the use of props are of utmost importance in these situations.

Play features that appeal to all ages and are used by the children according to their interests and skills are ideal for mixed age groups. Some ideas for shared space playgrounds are set out below.

- Sandpits are enjoyed by all children. If there is enough space it is useful to have a separate sandpit for the younger children as the boisterous play of older children often precludes the younger, more timid child. Props and toys suitable for the different age groups need to be added to the sand to cater for the differing interests.
- Swings with different attachments that can be changed throughout the day according to the skills of the children are a useful addition.
- Areas for dramatic play suit all ages and include low decking, bush cubbies, cubbyhouses, amphitheatres, fallen tree logs, a clump of tree stump seats, cosy corners around the playground. All these can be used with the addition of props such as furniture, dress-ups, picnic sets, pots and pans, paper and pencils, telephones etc. Simple dramatic play themes, such as putting a doll to bed, to more complex themes, such as hospital or office play, can engage children for many hours.
- Flat surfaces, such as lawn, paving, and verandah areas, are suitable for age-appropriate construction toys and blocks, as well as tabletop activities.

Many child-care centres with limited outdoor space tend to stagger the use of the outdoors so that the area can be set up either with activities to extend the older children, or toys and activities more suited to the babies and toddlers. The following scenarios describe how two country centres planned for their children's needs.

● 1. A preschool in a rural area was redeveloped to cater for the changing needs of the community. Occasional care was needed as more parents in the local community were employed, both as part-time and full-time workers, and the families and single parents needed respite care The centre serviced a large geographical area and the preschool fed nine different schools in the surrounding areas.

A new centre was built on the old site and included a child-care section and a sessional preschool section.

Staff and parents were involved in deciding the kind of play areas that would be suitable for an age range of birth to five, some in care, some in sessional preschool and some using both at different times. After much research and professional help, a design was drawn up that catered for the differing needs of the children.

The outdoor area was very large with a natural fall in the land and beautiful old trees providing many shady places. No divisions were made in the elongated playground. Play features for the younger children in child care were placed directly out from the door to the child-care section. A small cosy sandpit, swings and a cubbyhouse were all placed close to the building. The more confident children could wander into the rest of the playground, explore the garden area and the larger sandpit.

The playground for the older children included a very large sandpit with a watercourse, swings, a garden with a sensory path, a digging area, a vegetable garden, a dramatic play platform and a soft-fall area for movable climbing equipment. As the land sloped away steeply to the north, away from the child-care area, play features that were not appropriate for the very young were placed beyond the steep slope. These included areas such as swings, digging areas, and a grassed area suitable for running and ball games. Young babies were taken to this grassed area when the older children were inside.

Comments from staff in the centre included the fact that the area could accommodate large groups of children, the younger children could interact with older siblings outside and children had room to run and explore.

The Coordinator of the centre found that in an integrated setting such as this, it was most important that staff had shared goals and excellent communication. All staff needed to be flexible, believe in the benefits of an integrated program and be prepared to work with all the children.

2. A country primary school with approximately 200 students had quite a large playground with space for all the children. A preschool with age-appropriate equipment and play features shared a corner of the property. At recess time junior primary students would visit the preschool playground. Originally this was encouraged by staff as it allowed brothers and sisters to play together. However, over time the older children would come at recess time, with their fruit, climb to the top of the slide and stay there until the end of recess, others would sit on the play platform leaving no room for the younger children. There was in fact a complete 'takeover' by the older children.

Preschool staff noticed that the preschool children spent the whole of school recess time huddled together on bench seats along the side of the building, watching the older children but with no interaction between the two groups. This problem was raised at a staff meeting and the older children were banned from the area except in special circumstances. It was later discovered that there was insufficient seating for these junior primary students in their playground as the older primary students claimed all the seats at recess and lunchtime. More seating was placed around the playground and the junior primary students happily stayed in their own area. ●

Playgroups

Often parents with young children become isolated due to lack of time, money and family support. Young mothers often deny themselves time out from family responsibilities. However, playgroups are usually seen by parents as a legitimate outing, as they believe that their children will benefit from socialising with other children their own age and younger. Many lasting friendships are developed between parents who attend playgroups. In an area where there are families with no extended family nearby or single parents, playgroups fulfil an extremely valuable role in the wellbeing of the whole family.

Playgrounds often do not cater for adults who need to be near their children but would like to socialise with other adults at the same time. Garden seats in shady areas in the playground provide the parents with a place to sit while watching and interacting with both children and other adults. Many a centre staff member has been heard to say, 'I wish the parents would go outside with their children instead of staying inside gossiping'. In most cases the playground has no adult-sized seats in shady areas near where the children play to encourage parents to venture outside. Seats around a sandpit for example are most important as the sandpit is the most used area, especially for the younger children.

Some centres have the luxury of having an area especially for these younger children. Equipment designed specifically for younger children can then be installed. Equipment suitable for younger children is discussed in Chapter 4.

chapter 3 The planning process for the development of playgrounds

The information in this chapter aims to provide all those who work with and for children in an early childhood centre or school with an outline of a planning process that will assist them in developing a concept for a playground design. The information about drawing up a concept design is to enable centres to present a design to landscapers and contractors or for it to be used as a guide for working parties of volunteers or community groups. It will depend on how major a redevelopment is planned as to whether the whole planning process needs to be followed.

Clarify your goals

It is important to clarify the centre's goals for children attending the program. Ask all the staff working in the centre to outline what it is they would like the children to be able to do and achieve in the outdoors — the knowledge and skills they would like them to develop. Have them create a wish list of play features they would like; for example, a quiet area where children and staff can sit for fruit or a story, or a place where staff can pitch a tent with the children so that they can pretend they are camping.

As well as input from the staff, involve management committees or school councils, families, and the centre's community in all of the stages of development. Inform them of the problems with the present playground and the needs of the children.

If the centre has other groups using the area, such as playgroups, occasional care, or a creche, ask them what they would like their children to be able to do in the playground. Community involvement takes longer and it is not always easy, but handled sensitively it results in ownership and commitment, plus a boost in confidence and morale for all those who have made a contribution, however small. Tables 3.1, 3.2 and 3.3 illustrate some of the types of ideas your team may come up with.

TABLE 3.1 NOTES FROM A CHILD-CARE CENTRE'S TEAM MEETING

What would you like to see babies and toddlers doing in the outdoor environment?

ball games	dramatic play	hiding	painting	riding bikes	sitting	swinging
block play	eating	jumping	playing in the shade	riding horses	sliding	table activities
climbing	exploring	laughing	playing with sand	running	small group games	talking
crawling	having fun	listening to stories	playing with water	singing	smelling	walking on tracks

What would you like to see two- to five-year-old children doing in the outdoor play area?

balancing	experimenting with nature	laughing	sand & water play
bike riding	extension of indoor learning	learning about nature	sharing/taking turns
building & constructing	growing plants	marching	singing
camping	hammering	opportunities for solitary play	smelling
climbing	having fun	painting	swinging
co-operating	hide & seek	painting murals	tiptoeing
crawling/tunnelling	hopscotch	playing in small groups	treasure hunt
cutting & pasting	imaginative/dramatic play	problem solving	using shade
dancing	jumping	punching (punch bag)	using shelter
discovering	kicking balls	respecting equipment	walking backwards
experimenting (maths, science, music)	large group games	rolling	

TABLE 3.2 STAFF WISH LIST FOR A SCHOOL PLAYGROUND

- Things that children can hide behind, for example bushes or trees
- Line marking for hand tennis court
- A sandpit, one deep one for digging, one shallow one for car tracks
- More seats for having lunch

Empower all the groups to make appropriate decisions by having information sessions using visuals, such as photos, slides or videos, on the developmental needs of the children, and examples of other playgrounds and some of their play features. Discuss how children would use certain play features and the possible learning outcomes.

It is important that the whole centre community is working towards the same goals. Encourage staff, families and committees to visit other early childhood playgrounds that have been redeveloped and observe the children using play features similar to those likely to be chosen for their playground.

Ask them what they would like to see in the playground. Sometimes the suggestions may be unrealistic. Usually that is because they are looking at the playground as being the same as a local playground, which is for short-term use and mainly for recreation, rather than long-term use as part of the educational learning environment. However, often their suggestions, if not quite suitable, can be used as a starting point for discussion. Some valuable suggestions from parents are shown in Table 3.3.

TABLE 3.3 SOME IDEAS FROM PARENTS FOR OUTDOOR AREAS IN A CHILD-CARE CENTRE

- More shade in the nursery area
- Colourful shrubs and flowers for the children to smell
- Undulated surfaces
- Boat/pirate ship
- Sandpit with an island in the middle
- Windmill

If the children using the playground are of an age where they can draw or write about where they like to play, talk informally to them, being careful not to use the term playground but rather where they like to play, their interests at home and at school and ask them to write or draw a picture about it. Older children can write a wish list, draw a picture of their favourite place to play, or write an essay on what they like to do in their spare time. Accept every suggestion enthusiastically as they too can be a starting point for discussions.

If we use the word ‘playground’ children tend to think only of equipment such as swings, climbing structures and slides and seldom include mounds, bush cubbies, sand and plants. Although they play in and around these features they do not see them as part of a playground. However, if you ask children about their favourite place to play at weekends and holidays it is often climbing a tree, making a cubby in the bushes, damming up a creek with river stones or playing with sand and water at the beach. Tables 3.4 and 3.5 offer an insight into children's ideas for playgrounds.

TABLE 3.4 SCHOOL CHILDREN'S WISH LIST

- More trees around the oval so that there is more shade
- Bench seats as a divider between the older students' oval and the junior primary oval
- Rubbish bins around the oval so that they don't have to walk so far to put their rubbish in the bin
- Flowers to pick
- More things for girls to do
- Sand, water, mounds, bridges, somewhere for pretend/fantasy play
- An adventure area
- Somewhere to play with cars and dolls that they bring from home, a place to make tracks.

TABLE 3.5 PLAY FEATURES INCLUDED IN SCHOOL CHILDREN'S DRAWINGS

bridge	house
car tracks (in sand or soil)	dodgem cars
climbing equipment, which included: – mounds – flying fox – fire-fighters' pole – hanging rings – monkey bars – ropes and chains – tunnel – fort – ladders – trees – turn-over bars	garden grass hopscotch jungle kissing booth !!! sandpit shade slides swings
cubby	trampoline
fort	

For any project to be successful there must be ownership, no-one is particularly interested in looking after the maintenance of a playground, watering plants, and mowing lawns unless they were part of the development process. Contributors may have grown some of the plants from cuttings or helped plant the lawn, they may have been part of the committee who made the final choices of play features to be included in the new playground. All those who have input in the decision-making develop a feeling of ownership.

School playgrounds are usually organised quite differently to early childhood centres such as child-care centres and preschools. The playgrounds tend to be used mainly for recreational purposes. However, there are an increasing number of schools that are now using their outdoor areas to provide experiences for the students that are part of their curriculum. Curriculum areas such as Society and Environment, Science and Technology, Health and Physical Education, English, Mathematics and The Arts and Aboriginal Studies can all be incorporated in playground design. Table 3.6 lists some ways that teachers have sought to incorporate curriculum with the playground equipment.

TABLE 3.6 STAFF WISH LIST FOR AREAS THAT COULD BE USED AS AN EXTENSION TO THE CURRICULUM

- ant farm
- barbecue area
- bird bath
- class gardens
- flowers
- garden for native and non-native plants
- pergola with table & chairs for outdoor lessons in:
  - science
  - art
  - drama
  - music
- pond for frogs and fish
- pond with waterfall
- quiet withdrawal area
- trees and paths
- vegetable patch
- worm farm

Draw up a list of who will be using the playground

Record how many children are likely to use the playground at any one time, their ages, when and how often they will attend, their needs, problems, and constraints.

Take note of any specific needs such as children with disabilities, Aboriginal or Torres Strait Islander children, children from other cultures, and those attending with or without adults.

Staff in early childhood centres have observed that Indigenous Australian children are extremely agile and require much more challenging physical experiences. A research project carried out in 1972 by Prescott, Jones and Kritchevsky found children from higher socioeconomic families tended to prefer open spaces. When placed in crowded playgrounds conflicts arose; whereas, children from low socioeconomic families or warm, large extended family cultures enjoyed crowded space where many children shared the same space without conflict.

If the playground development is for a new centre it is important to become familiar with the needs of the community. Do the children come from an area where there are high-rise units, where there is little opportunity for physical activities such as running, jumping, climbing? Do the children know how to play? Are they used to mixing with other children? Is there a mix of cultural backgrounds and do those cultures have very different child-rearing customs?

Carry out an analysis of the proposed or existing playground

Table 3.7 illustrates the type of areas that will need to be investigated in your playground analysis.

If there is already a playground on the site, document why the area needs redeveloping. Many of the above factors will be known already, such as whether there is a drainage problem or not and where it is.

Look at existing play features and decide what needs to stay and what needs to go. Plan around the items that are to stay, remove or mend all dangerous equipment or landscape features. Is something appropriate but in the wrong place? Can it be repositioned or part of it recycled? Sometimes it is useful to look at the area as though nothing is there and do a rough sketch of what would be in the ideal playground and would suit the needs of all the children.

If there is a dispute over what is to be removed, do an observation of children's use of that play feature. Use independent observers, such as high school students or trainee teachers, to record how long and how many children or boys or girls use the structure during outdoor playtime. Record the use over a week, or once every week on different days for five to six weeks, taking into account that the use may be influenced by program changes from day to day; for example, children going to the library every Thursday lunchtime.

TABLE 3.7 ANALYSIS OF PLAYGROUND

Factor	Analysis
Climate	Is it a hot dry climate or is it cold and wet?
Natural environment	Are there natural slopes, mounds, creeks, trees? It is important to make use of these features unless they present a safety risk to the children.
Wind	Is there a time of the year when prevailing winds are particularly strong?
Rain	Is it a high rainfall area or low? This will affect the choice of plants. Wind and rain comes from the same direction in most areas although there are climates that are less predictable and the weather can come from several directions.
Soil	Is it good fertile soil or does it need fertilisers or mulching?
Sun	The angle of the sun varies not only from morning to afternoon but from summer to winter. The areas of sun and shade in both winter and summer need to be recorded so that maximum use can be made of both sunny and shady positions. Shade structures can then be positioned appropriately and gardens can be planted with either sun- or shade- loving plants.
Space available	Do you need to think small when choosing play features or can undulating mounds be accommodated?
Drainage	Is there an area where water lies and does not drain away? If so, this will need to be addressed before any redevelopment can take place. Professional help may be required.
Plumbing and other underground services	Where are these positioned? You will need to contact the supply authorities or councils. It can be prove to be very expensive if permanent structures are erected over underground services.
Positioning	The position of fences, gates, paths, doors and windows on the buildings and any storage sheds needs to be recorded.
Adult and child traffic	How adults and children move through the area impacts on any plan. Often grass will indicate where people cut corners as the lawn is withered, non-existent, looks very worn or plants in the corner of a garden bed never seem to thrive.
Access for emergency services and trucks delivering soft-fall materials	You will need to allow space for these vehicles to enter the playground.

Play features should fit your needs

Choose play features that fit with the needs and requirements of your particular centre. Work out what play features are to be included. Make sure there is a variety of play options covering all the developmental areas. For example, ensure there is a variety of physical play options rather than many climbing experiences. Go back to the list compiled by staff of what they would like the children to be able to do in the outdoors. Check that all developmental areas are well covered; for example, have they considered the emotional needs of the children, have they included areas for socialising? Do not choose a particular play feature just because another centre has one. It may not be appropriate for your site or community.

If children have spent a great deal of time playing on the climbing structure, they may then want a quiet place to play with a few friends. Have you provided for that? If you have children who engage in sustained socio-dramatic play, have you provided enough areas for that to happen? Have you provided enough empty space for children to run, construct, and play ball games?

Record the path of child traffic through the playground

Children always take the shortest possible route to any play feature they wish to use. If a cement or paved path is not the most direct route to where they want to go they will not use it. They will cut corners and walk over gardens. If the path or verandah has too many obstacles on it, for example, tables, and equipment, they will not use it. However, if the obstacles are small, such as construction toys or train sets on a mat, they will run through the centre of the play and out the other side, disrupting other children. So it is important to take note of where the children go. If movable climbing equipment is placed in front of a piece of equipment, make sure that there is still a space left at the side of the movable equipment and the fixed equipment so that children can see their way clear to get through to other play features.

When positioning a play-platform, cubbyhouse or amphitheatre, or any other structure that has an entrance in the playground, make sure that the entrance is in line with where the children are most likely to run, particularly with children under five years. If a structure doesn't invite them in as they pass, they will not think of going behind or to the side to enter. The entrance needs to be clearly visible from the main child traffic flow. If it is a new centre playground and children have not yet had a chance to use it, try and look at where the children are most likely to run, and place an opening where it can be easily seen. Remember the sandpit is the most used, so the children will run straight from the centre's exit door to the sandpit. The most direct route does not need to have a hard surface path, particularly if it would cut the playground in half. If a hard surface path needs to go to the sandpit because of children with disabilities or for ease of staff carrying equipment, maybe the sandpit would be better placed to one side.

Draw up a concept design

If a site plan is already available this can be reproduced to a larger scale that will give you the layout of the area complete with the sizes. If no plans are available measure the boundaries accurately with a tape measure of five to ten metres or even longer and create your own site plan. Take the measurements of the length and breadth of the block. Unless the block is an irregular shape it is best to measure across the middle of the block. Determine where north is and place it at the top of the plan.

Draw the plan to scale on graph paper using scales of 1:200, 1:100 or 1:50, which are scales commonly used by designers and landscapers. Make several copies of the site plan. If the block is an irregular shape and too difficult to measure, it may pay to have the site surveyed so that you and the final landscaper or contractor can use the survey plan.

Locate the position and size of the centre's building on the block. Show the doors from the buildings and all sheds. Measure and record the position of all the trees and any significant shrubs as well as any existing paths that are to remain. Include all existing landscaping and play features that are to be included in the new plan. Use all the existing trees on the site unless they are in a place where other play options need to be placed. Try not to remove any trees as they take such a long time to grow and their benefits to the playground and the environment as a whole are invaluable.

Find out the size and shape of the new play features. Make templates of those features and place them on the concept design where you imagine they might be best suited. Use trees, or screening plants to block out any strong winds and to provide shade in the appropriate places. Check with information in Chapter 1 as to suggested placement of some of the play features.

Draw up the concept design with all the new play features and landscaping included and present it to the decision-makers. When the design has been approved it is then ready for the landscapers, and/or contractors to assume the responsibility of the project. However, it is advisable that the decision-makers ensure their final requests are adhered to, as some contractors may not understand the reasons behind the choice of features or why they must be where the centre wants them. For those centres engaging in small changes to their play environment, the concept design can be copied and used by working parties.

It is important to remember that all constructions must adhere to the Australian Standards on Playground Surfacing (1996) and Playgrounds and Playground Equipment Part 1 (1997), particularly in regard to the safety aspects. (See Chapter 1 for contact number.) All contractors and builders need to be familiar with these standards. It is also important to check with your local authorities if their approval is required before commencement of construction.

Outline stages of development

Compile a staged report outlining an order of development that will minimise disruption to the centre and children who still need to use the area during the redevelopment. For example, all earth-moving projects should be carried out first. If a new sandpit is to be installed, and the centre's program has to operate during redevelopment, do not move the old one until the new one is in and operating as this is the most used play area in early childhood centres.

Record the process and the reasons for the changes and choice of play features so that staff and committees that follow on will understand why particular play features were chosen and not immediately want to change things. Too many new committees and staff want to change what is often a very good playground.

However, some do not want to change anything, even when it is dangerous or worn out. Staff and committees change from year to year and it is useful for them to be able to follow on with the next stage early in their appointment so that they can complete a section and gain a sense of achievement.

Creating a concept design

To illustrate a concept design we'll use an example from a community centre that operates a child-care service and many playgroups. The children are aged from six months to five years old and those at playgroup attend with their parents at various times throughout the week. There is also a creche for children whose parents attend classes at the centre from time to time. The building was not purpose-built but is an old hall that has been converted into a community centre.

A copy of the initial rough site plan is shown in Figure 3.1.

It is important to understand that this design is only suitable for this particular location and group of children and would not be appropriate in any other location. However, the design and explanations may be useful in understanding how important the placement of features and the play behaviour of children are when designing a children's playground.

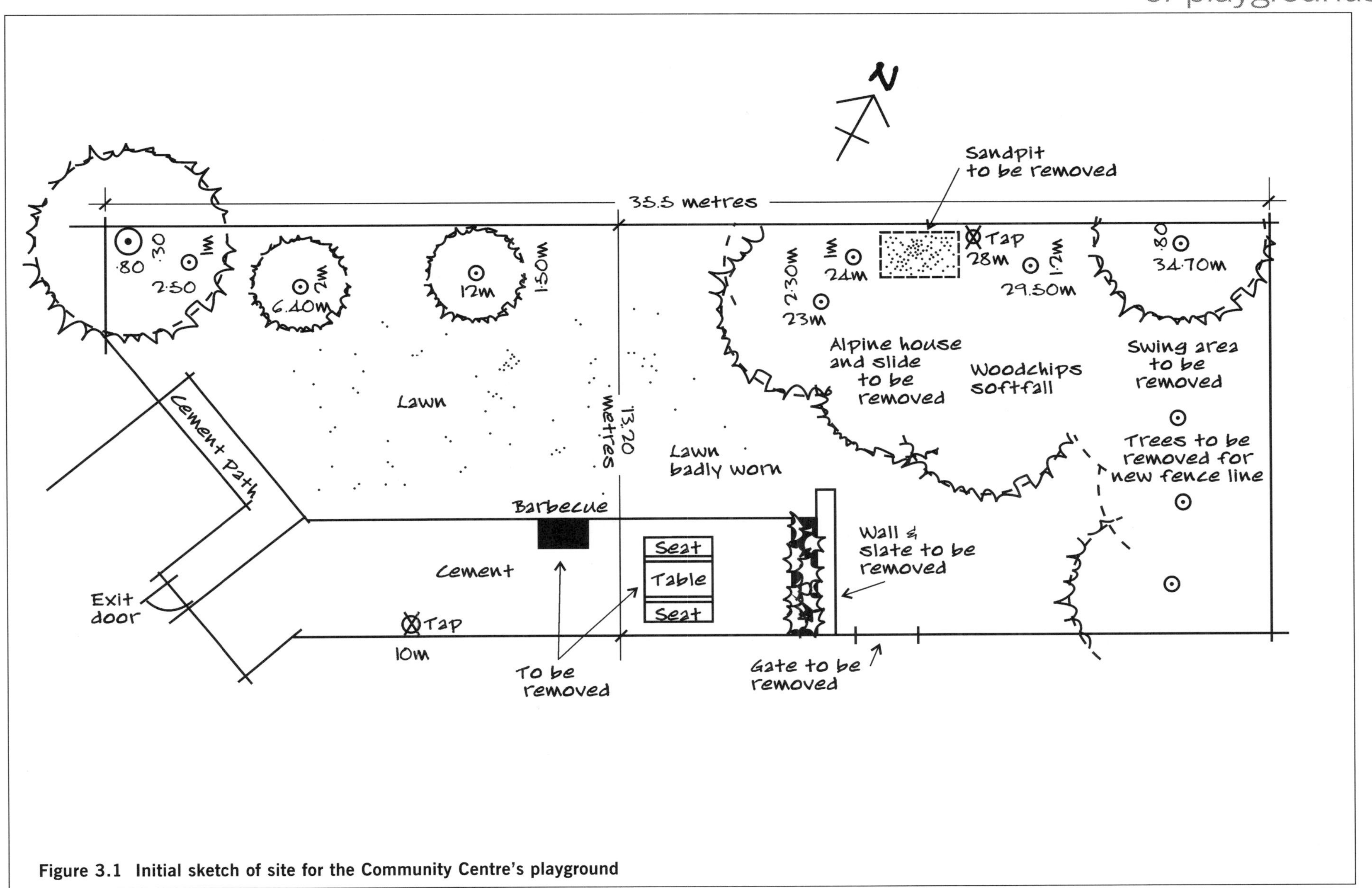

Figure 3.1 Initial sketch of site for the Community Centre's playground

The basic plan had the following features:

- A site plan was available, several enlarged copies were made of the playground area, some to be used as rough copies.
- All underground services were already marked on the site plan and were positioned on the other side of the building away from the playground area. The water piping ran along the northern fence line and was not in the way of any excavations.
- The size of the playground measured. 35.55 m W/E × 13.20 m N/S.
- The position of existing trees was marked on the initial rough plan (for example, 2.50 m W/E × 1 m N/S) as well as the position of paths and the location of taps. The reason for measuring these features is to ensure that when placing templates of play features on the plan they will fit and trees and paths do not have to be repositioned (see Figure 3.1). The position of shade in summer and winter, and where the lawn grew and where it didn't was also marked on the plan.

The original playground had a swing, a very small sandpit and an alpine house on stilts with a slide that needed replacing attached to one side. The whole centre was to be revamped, some of the fence lines were to be altered and money was available to upgrade the playground through fundraising and grants.

On the eastern end there were shady trees and on the western end very little shade and a lawn that became swamped when it rained due to poor drainage. The lawn did not grow on the southern side due to heavy wear and tear of children's feet as they ran from the door of the building to the eastern end where the swing, slide and sandpit were located.

The staff identified some problem areas as:

- no covered/dry areas in winter;
- an old wall next to the slate driveway presents a danger to children who may climb up on top of it and fall onto the slate;
- difficulty keeping any garden alive;
- wasted areas, particularly under some of the trees; and
- a fixed table under the pergola prevents the staff and children using the area for anything else.

As the staff had noted, there were large areas of the playground that were not fully utilised including the old slate driveway, a heavily shaded area with large tree roots protruding above the ground, the cemented area in front of the building which had no shelter and a brick barbecue and fixed picnic table that obstructed the child traffic flow through the area, and the lawn area, which was either too hot in summer or too wet underfoot in winter.

Staff brainstormed what they would like the children to be able to do in the playground, and the playgroup was asked what they would like to have in the playground. Wish lists were compiled and a rough concept was drawn up for all parties to consider. The staff wish list is shown in Table 3.8. A few changes were made then the final concept design was drawn up to be given to the developers to be used as a guide.

TABLE 3.8 STAFF WISH LIST
amphitheatre
area to sit/talk/read/have group time
atmosphere
bicycle path (surface to ride/push/pull)
bridge
comfortable adult area
larger sandpit
natural features
open area for physical activity
plants that survive/thrive
raised platforms
shed on fence line
swings (2 × changeable attachments)
target on wall
verandah (covered in)
water play

The concept design is shown in Figure 3.2. (The concept design was originally drawn up on a scale of 1:100 but it has been reduced for publication.)

In the north-eastern corner a low jetty and boat was erected. This centre is near a railway line and trains periodically pass by. Consequently, children run to the fence to watch the trains. The jetty doubles as a watching place for trains. A winding path of compacted sand leads children towards the boat, crossing over a bridge and through perfumed plants.

The slate area and the old wall were removed and a bike track was put in their place, beginning with an archway from the cement path to encourage children to ride through the archway onto the track. The outside of the oval track is flat and suitable for children who are beginning to ride a tricycle or to use push–pull toys. The centre path has a low gently sloping bridge and a rumble strip in it to increase the difficulty and offer a challenge to those children who are proficient riders. This area is in partial shade at times but mainly full sun.

A low long mound separates the bike track and the exploratory area. Hardy native shrubs have been planted on the mound to soften the area and act as a deterrent to bike riders who might stray from the track. In between the mound and the winding path several trees have been planted with tree stump seats placed in the shade of the trees.

As most gardens need sun to thrive, a children's garden was established in the centre of the bike track, where it is always sunny, with tree trunk rounds as a path leading from one section to another. Screening plants along the fence line offer the children privacy from the street as they play.

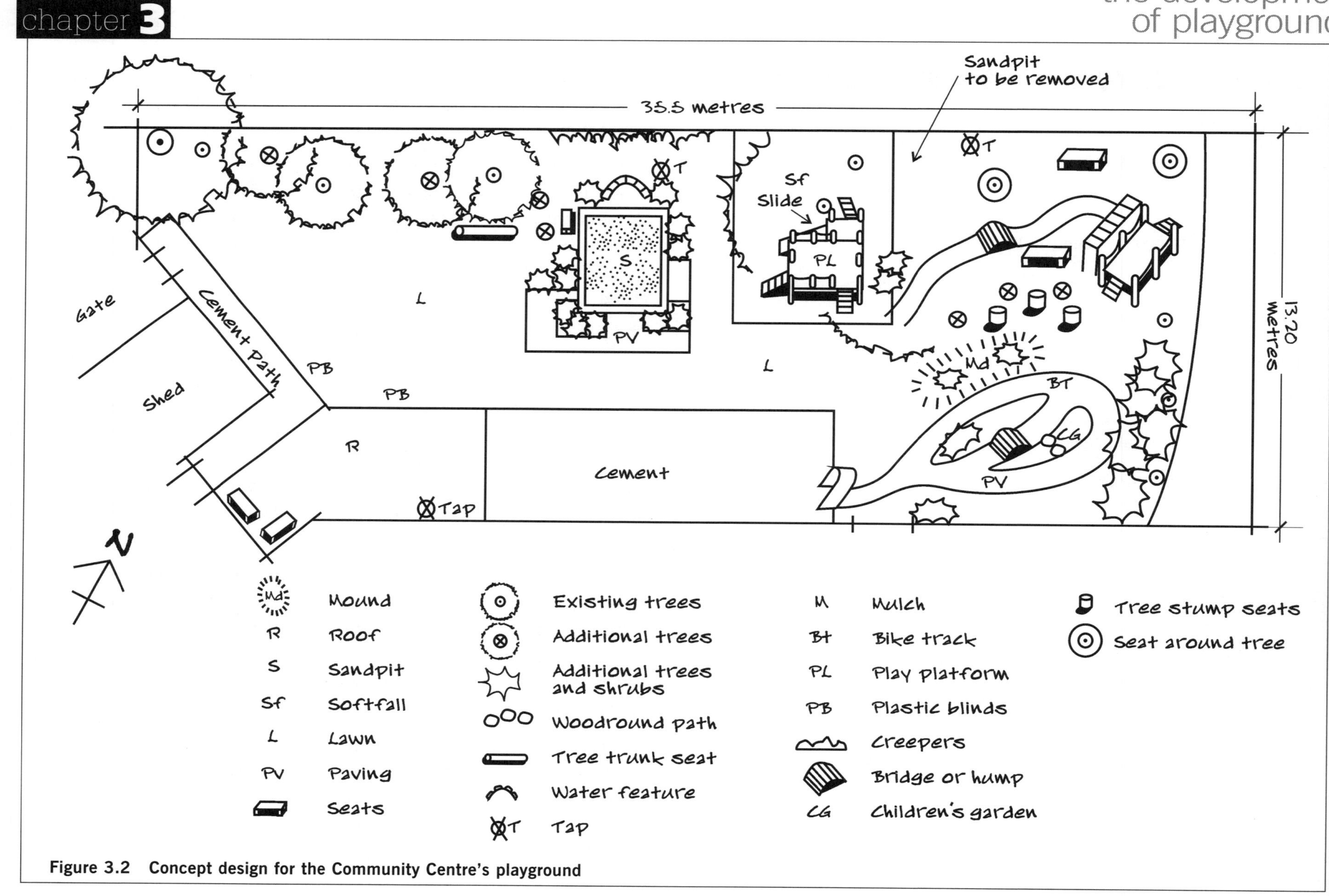

Figure 3.2 Concept design for the Community Centre's playground

The north-eastern end of the playground is in continual shade and the leaf litter makes it very difficult to grow any plants. This is an ideal place to put play features that require woodchips soft-fall. The area was excavated to take the soft-fall bringing the level up to ground level and eliminating the trip hazards of raised edgings.

In front of the exploratory area is a two-sectioned play platform. The small platform is high enough for a slide to be attached. Steps up to the slide are in a position so that children can move from the sandpit onto the steps and slide. Children who have had a slide can run back to the steps and have another slide without colliding with children from the other platform section. The larger platform is low, approximately 300 mm and has galvanised piping in timber posts across the front at a height of 500 mm and 800 mm so that movable boards and ladders can be attached when appropriate (see an example in Figure 6.1). Steps up from the western side allow for children to leave the sandpit by the eastern path and move onto the play platform. Staff need to place furniture and props such as dress-ups or picnic plates, cups and utensils or even construction toys in the area to ensure children use the platform. An empty platform has little appeal to children, it is just an empty space.

A sandpit approximately 4 m × 3 m was positioned just west of the permanently shaded area with a pergola over it. It is at ground level to reduce the possibility of children tripping over raised edges. Garden beds are placed around the sandpit to give the area a cosy feel and to reduce the areas where children can leave the sandpit. This is to reduce the build up of sand all around the edge.

There are three paths leaving the sandpit and they are of non-slip pavers. Sand can be swept back into the sandpit from these paths. Each path is designed to lead children into another play area or to provide a direct route to the building. The path on the southern side of the sandpit is wider than the others to cater for the child traffic flow from the lawn area to the soft-fall areas in an attempt to reduce the wear and tear on the lawn. A bench seat is positioned in the north-west corner for staff and carers to sit on while interacting with children playing in the sand. A water feature, which supplies running water into the sandpit, is on the northern side and is controlled by a vandal-proof tap. The water drains straight into the sandpit with no pools or puddles that young children could fall in.

North-west of the sandpit several extra trees have been planted to create a bush cubby and a tree trunk seat has been placed in the area.

The poor drainage was addressed by the developers and the area is now available for children to crawl, run, jump or play ball games.

The barbecue and the fixed picnic table and seat were removed providing another hard surface area where children can play ball, rugs can be placed on the floor and construction toys or puzzles can be set up when appropriate.

A sitting area with a roof over the exit door now provides staff and children with the opportunity to use the area for stories, songs, morning tea or to be set up as a home corner. Clear heavy-duty plastic blinds have been placed along the front of the roofed area to protect the children from the wind and rain, particularly in the winter.

An existing shed has been re-positioned so that it opens out onto the edge of the playground on the western end, reducing the distance staff have to carry equipment, and the existing cement path has been extended along in front of the shed.

The existing watering system was upgraded to include the extra garden areas and new trees to ensure that plants did not die due to lack of water.

Factors that contribute to unsuccessful playgrounds

The following factors can make playgrounds unsuccessful:

1. Decision-makers not looking closely at all the developmental needs of children.
2. Decision-makers not planning the play area as a whole and having no overall plan.
3. Decision-makers choice influenced by attractive glossy brochures rather than needs.
4. Centres spending large amounts of hard to find funds on inappropriate equipment such as that which is not age-appropriate or a type that duplicated the experience already provided by another piece of equipment ie climbing equipment.
5. Very few centres budget for outdoor areas so they make do with a tired and/or badly maintained playground.
6. Playgrounds that provide only for the children's physical needs.
7. Little to no provision for the type of play features than promote sustained play.
8. Little to no provision for children's dramatic play.
9. Not enough to do per child (Kritchevsky et al. 1977)
10. Nothing that promotes curiosity. No interesting paths, bridges and sensory walks to explore. Barren play areas or those with gardens that are so precious children can only look but not touch.
11. Very little to no use of plants and shrubs or natural features in the environment.
12. No attention given to the natural flow of child traffic through the playground.
13. Good features in the wrong position or with the exit/access points in the wrong place.
14. Features that were in the right position and were age-appropriate, but staff didn't know how to use them; for example, dramatic play platforms need props and furniture.
15. Inappropriate landscaping such as large mounds in front of swings so that the swings are out of sight to the children, or swings placed in the middle of the play area so that children run through the swing area on their way to other areas.

chapter 4 Outdoor areas for children under two years

> Neuroscientists have found that throughout the entire process of development — beginning even before birth — the brain is affected by environmental conditions … The impact of the environment is dramatic and specific, not merely influencing the general direction of development, but actually affecting how the intricate circuitry of the brain is 'wired'.
>
> (Shore 1997, p. 15)

With advances in technology scientists are discovering more and more about how the human brain works. No longer do they believe that the brain develops according to the genes we have but rather a combination of inherited genes and experiences.

According to Shore (1997, p. 21) 'By the age of two, toddlers brains are as active as those of adults, and by three they are two-and-a-half times as active', which suggests the early childhood years are a prime time for learning. This new information supports what early childhood educators have believed all along — that the experiences and environments we provide for young children are of utmost importance.

The outdoor area for children under two needs to be both interesting and safe, one where children with the support of their caregivers can use all their senses to explore their environment and discover whether they can change what they see, hear or feel through their own actions. Wortham and Wortham (1989, p. 299) have said: 'Since sensory exploration is one of the most important play experiences for the infant and toddler, the environment needs to be highly interactive of the five senses.'

The addition of props or loose parts is important to provide the variety required to cater for all the interests and needs of the children. An environment where 'nothing needs to be added' would cause children to lose interest. Interests change very quickly at this stage because children are rapidly passing from one developmental stage to the next. Table 4.1 outlines characteristics of young babies that should be kept in mind when planning a playground.

Young babies (birth to six months)

Although the outdoor play area is not as important at this stage as later in their development, there are still experiences in the outdoors that can enrich the lives of small babies. Table 4.1 illustrates this.

TABLE 4.1 YOUNG BABIES (BIRTH TO SIX MONTHS) USE THEIR SENSES TO LEARN ABOUT THE WORLD AROUND THEM

- They are very interested in things that move slowly, and follow them with their eyes.
- They begin to use their hands and mouths to explore their feet and objects within their reach, grasping and holding onto things.
- They are attracted to things that make gentle sounds.
- In the early stages, they are frightened by sudden movements and loud noises.
- They seek out adults for play, holding out their arms to be picked up.

In the early months of a baby's life the relationship with adults is of prime importance and staff need to be warm, caring and supportive. Playful interactions between babies and their caregivers can provide support for the development of social skills. The sensorimotor play of babies occurs less often when they are alone than with a caring playful adult.

A garden environment with shady trees provides leaves that move, flutter and rustle in the breeze and a place to hang mobiles and wind chimes. Australian native trees such as callistemons, grevilleas and banksias attract nectar-feeding birds, and eucalypts attract seed-eaters. The playground could be full of a variety of birds for children to see and hear. Placing bird feeders outside a window in a quiet section of the playground or garden provides another opportunity for children to observe birds.

Planting a variety of hardy flowering plants such as geraniums, lavender, rosemary and other herbs provides colour to attract the children's attention as well as softening the play environment.

Check with your local botanic gardens for information on poisonous plants.

A shaded grassy area is useful for adults to place a rug and cushions for immobile babies to lie on, where staff can interact with the babies as they watch the clouds float gently across the sky, see the birds fly past and feel the breeze on their skin. Placing babies in different positions around the playground provides them with a variety of sensory experiences.

Bench seats in the playground encourage staff to sit in the garden while they are nursing the babies; they provide a place for staff and babies to watch and interact with each other.

There needs to be a safe area away from the toddlers to place immobile babies so that they can roll over, lie on their tummies and attempt to crawl. Most child-care centres have verandahs where soft carpet squares can be rolled out and cushions scattered about for the young babies to lie and where adults can sit and cuddle babies. Textured blankets placed over the carpet for babies to explore gives them a tactile experience of the different textures.

It is useful to have a section of the verandah that can be divided from the rest of the play areas with removable soft fencing made of canvas or some similar material with thick clear plastic window inserts to allow children to see out into the playground. This fencing can be tied to the verandah posts when required. It provides a quiet place for small babies and reduces the likelihood of accidents with older toddlers falling over the babies.

Suggestions for staff

Table 4.2 is designed to provide staff with some ideas to facilitate the development of children in the birth to six month age group.

TABLE 4.2 SUGGESTIONS FOR STAFF WORKING WITH BABIES BIRTH TO SIX MONTHS

- Walk around the playground with the baby and talk about what you can see.
- Place a mobile or wind chimes in a nearby tree, listen to the sounds with the baby, talk about them.
- Watch leaves flutter in the trees.
- Nurse the baby, rock backwards and forwards while you sing a song or listen to music.
- Nurse the baby and look at a book together. Make sure the pictures are large, clear and are of familiar objects. Talk about what you both can see in the book.
- Dance with the baby in your arms while you are singing.
- Sit the baby on your lap facing you so that the baby can watch your mouth as you talk.
- Put the baby on a rug in the garden where he/she can see staff and children, talk to the baby about what the children are doing.
- Give the baby soft cuddly toys, rattles, squeeze toys, toys of different textures and objects to grasp and feel.
- Play ‘this little pig’ with the baby’s fingers and toes, wriggling them as you talk.
- Allow the baby to push his/her feet against your hands, gently push back.

Babies (six to 12 months)

As babies become more mobile they begin to explore their immediate environment, as seen in Table 4.3.

TABLE 4.3 BABIES (SIX TO 12 MONTHS) MAY HAVE THE FOLLOWING CHARACTERISTICS
• begin to sit up, crawl, pull themselves up to stand
• may stand alone
• begin to walk holding onto something
• are interested in contents of cupboards, boxes etc.
• enjoy putting objects into containers and emptying them out
• delight in knocking over stacked blocks
• enjoy watching the rolling motion of balls, and pushing balls
• are interested in water and floating toys
• drag things along, and push and pull toys
• enjoy being pushed in swings
• climb over low obstacles
• are attracted to movement and sounds
• engage in simple pretend play

Safety is of prime importance at this age as everything goes into their mouths. Staff need to be vigilant to ensure that the area is free of hazards.

Staff need to interact with the children as they play in a warm, caring, supportive manner while they explore the outdoor environment. Look at the leaves and flowers in the garden together, feel the bark on the trees and draw the children's attention to birds or anything else that might be of interest in the outdoors. Talk to the children about what they are experiencing as these conversations are important for babies' and toddlers' language development.

The recently-mobile babies need a safe environment with soft surfaces such as grass to cushion their falls and low grassed undulations to crawl up and down. They need a flat grassy area when they begin to walk. Grass, however, is an extremely difficult surface for children to use push–pull toys.

As children of this age do not venture far away from the building or the adults, a path needs to be provided near the building for children to use push and pull toys. It is important that they are given these opportunities as they need to use their muscles so they can grow stronger.

Although these children enjoy swinging, a great deal of care must be taken if swings are provided (see section on swings in Chapter 1). It is most important that the surface under the swing is impact-absorbent. Small loose particles such as wood chips are inappropriate as at this age babies tend to put a lot of things into their mouths.

Pretend play at this stage usually requires single objects, such as a handbag, doll or telephone, all of which can be provided by staff when appropriate. Staff may need to model the appropriate actions.

Suggestions for staff

Table 4.4 is designed to provide staff with some ideas to facilitate the development of children in the six to 12 month age group.

TABLE 4.4 SUGGESTIONS FOR STAFF WORKING WITH BABIES SIX TO 12 MONTHS

- Put the baby on a rug on the grass or on a carpet on the verandah.
- Put objects on the rug that he/she can pick up, pull apart; include containers that can be filled and emptied, objects that can be grasped and explored.
- Allow the baby to see your face when you talk and make eye contact with the baby when you talk.
- Talk about what is in the garden, leaves on the trees, flowers, the weather and link it with clear pictures in a book.
- Act as a model for the baby, stack blocks in front of the baby, nurse a baby doll, feed the doll, put the doll to bed, stir a spoon in a pan.
- Play peek-a-boo.
- Hold the baby up and allow the baby to use his/her feet as a support.
- Hold the baby up and allow him/her to feel the sand and the grass with his/her toes.
- Allow the baby to crawl on grass, crawl with the baby.
- Build a low mound with cushions on the grass or carpet and encourage the baby to climb up the mound, or use a grassy mound in the playground if one is available

Make sure no part is small enough to go into the mouth.

Toddlers (12–18 months)

Once toddlers at 12–18 months have mastered walking they become very mobile, exploring everything around them. Table 4.5 lists some of the developmental areas for this age group.

TABLE 4.5 ACTIVITIES FOR TODDLERS (12–18 MONTHS)

- They like to climb
- Enjoy rolling, kicking and throwing balls
- Walk up stairs with help, steps with handrails
- Push–pull toys, carts, prams etc., ride-on bikes (no pedals)
- Explore tunnels
- Enjoy rockers
- Feel the differences in taste, smell and temperature

- Use spoons, buckets and spades, funnels, and colanders to scoop
- Explore without putting things in their mouths
- Enjoy natural outdoor things, such as plants, birds, insects, worms, animals
- Enjoy water play
- Engage in pretend play with a variety of props

A good playground addition for toddlers is a firm-surfaced path that winds through a garden area and provides toddlers with the opportunity to explore and discover a variety of exciting things. It is important for children to be able to touch, feel, and pick the different textured leaves and flowers. It also provides a place to drag, pull and push wheeled toys.

Children at this age also need a grassed area to push and kick large balls; climb into empty boxes and wriggle through soft tunnels; climb on, into, under and through equipment.

Staff must support toddlers as they explore their environment to ensure they are always safe:

● William (14 months) crawled up the ramp of the low play platform, he looked through the rails around the edge of the platform then climbed down and walked unsteadily towards the swings. A staff member sat on a bench seat next to the swings nursing a baby. William clambered up onto the seat next to the staff member who put her arm around William as he sat next to her watching the children having a swing. ●

Toddlers enjoy being pushed gently in a swing by an adult they trust. However, the swing area needs to be located away from the entry/exit doors of the building and from the main play area to reduce the possibility of young children walking into a moving swing. Children at this age do not look where they are going and tend to study the ground in front of them as they walk.

A shaded sandpit provides children with sensory experiences and the opportunity to scoop sand, put objects into buckets and knock down sandcastles. Language development is enhanced when staff members interact with the children helping them make sense of what they are experiencing. It is useful to provide seating for staff on one side of the sandpit so that they can sit and interact with the children as they play in the sand.

It is important that a seat for staff members at the side of a sandpit does not place them in a position where their backs are to the rest of the playground as staff always need to have a watchful eye on the whole playground.

A low play platform with a ramp access or cubbyhouse (see Chapter 1) with a table and several chairs provides an area where children engage in simple pretend play, talking on a telephone, using plastic picnic cups and plates, wearing hats, carrying bags, putting dolls to bed. Access to the cubby could be either by a ramp or several steps.

A miniature amphitheatre of two tiers (see Chapter 1) doubles as a seat as well as a place for children to climb up with help — an exercise that helps strengthen their leg muscles. The back of the amphitheatre could have a variety of herbs planted as a screen or it could be mounded to allow children to walk or climb down the gentle slope.

A paved area close to the building where a low table can be placed for finger painting and other art activities is also very useful.

Suggestions for staff

Table 4.6 shows activities staff can explore with toddlers.

TABLE 4.6 SUGGESTIONS FOR STAFF WORKING WITH TODDLERS (12–18 MONTHS)

- Place a rug on the grass, sit and look at books with the children. Talk about the pictures. Allow the children to walk away if they are not interested or when they lose interest.
- Make sure the area is safe for the children to explore.
- Play ball with the children, roll it to them and encourage them to roll it back to you.
- Give the children lots of time to practise their walking.
- Give them push–pull toys such as carts with objects that can be put in the cart.
- Give them some ride-on toys (with no pedals).
- Provide some large cardboard boxes the children can climb in and out of.
- Blow bubbles for the children to chase.
- Set up an obstacle course of soft objects for the children to clamber over, under, through, around, and ones they can roll down. A low grassy mound would be ideal for this activity.
- Set up a home corner on the verandah or under a tree with table, chairs, cups, saucers, plates and spoons and maybe hats and handbags etc.
- Model stirring a saucepan, having a cup of tea, sweeping a path. Talk about what is happening and encourage the children to join in.
- Sit in the sandpit and encourage the children to pour and fill containers with sand and/or water.
- Place some shells in the sandpit for the children to discover.
- Provide jugs and containers for children to pour water.
- Provide watering cans and access to a tap for children to water the plants.
- Dance, sing and move to music with the children.

If using water make sure the use of water is only with adult supervision and the containers are emptied before staff leave the area.

Toddlers (18–24 months)

Toddlers in this age group explore their environment and test their developing skills. Table 4.7 lists some of the developmental areas for this age group.

TABLE 4.7 ACTIVITIES ENJOYED BY TODDLERS (18–24 MONTHS)
• Throw a ball
• Push and pull carts around
• Sit in carts or on ride-on toys (with no pedals)
• Use a spoon to scoop
• Roll a ball, may roll it back to another
• Stack blocks
• Copy housework
• Walk on a wide balance board
• Try to balance on one foot
• Run fast
• Have no idea of consequences, may move into the path of a child pushing a pram
• Enjoy sand and water
• Try to jump and climb
• Learn through exploration
• Are interested in animals, insects, plants, birds, worms etc.
• Play by self, initiate play
• Imitate adult behaviours in play
• Engage in pretend play with more complexity
• Help put things away

Children at 18–24 months are steadier on their feet and are ready to run, jump up and down, and balance on wide edges. They need hard surfaces for pushing and pulling wheeled toys and soft surfaces for running, jumping and rolling (see Figure 4.1). They need a variety of levels for climbing safely, slides and large muscle equipment that is age-appropriate.

Low gently sloped mounds provide the opportunity to climb without the fear of falling. Children enjoy climbing to the top of raised areas to watch activities from a safe distance:

● Rebecca (19 months) sat on the top of the low mound watching the children and a staff member playing in the sandpit on the other side of the playground. The staff member said, 'let's sing some songs'. She made a cradle with her arms and began to sing 'Miss Polly had a Dolly'. All the children joined in. From a distance Rebecca quietly folded her arms to make a cradle and began to rock backwards and forwards. ●

Young children enjoy boxes where they can put objects or climb into themselves and they love being pulled around in a cart by an adult, often calling for more until the adult tires.

A level area either grassed or a hard surface with a mat is useful for simple construction toys such as blocks so that they can stack the blocks, if only to knock them down again.

The provision of small baskets, handbags, purses and carry bags will always be appreciated as they enjoy carrying things from one place to another.

Children at this age and stage are less likely to put things in their mouths and will spend considerable time in a sanded area where they can fill and empty buckets with sand, using scoops and spades. Extra sand toys, such as trucks, boats and sieves are useful adjuncts. Water play in buckets in the sandpit will give children the opportunity to pour and stir.

Provide the children with watering cans so that they can water the garden — this way they will become more aware of the natural elements around them.

All activities using water must be well supervised and containers emptied prior to adults leaving the area.

Figure 4.1 Toddlers using push–pull toys

Suggestions for staff

Table 4.8 provides staff with some ideas to facilitate the development of children in the 18–24 months age group.

TABLE 4.8 SUGGESTIONS FOR STAFF WORKING WITH TODDLERS (18–24 MONTHS)
• Place a rug on the grass and read a picture book with the children. Show the children pictures of flowers, trees, birds and any other familiar objects they may see in the playground.
• Sing favourite songs while sitting on the rug.
• Talk about what other children are doing in the playground.
• Copy the sounds you can hear outside, encourage the children to do the same.
• Walk around the garden and name all the things the children can see; talk about those things to the children

- Provide the children with a variety of balls of different sizes and textures. Play ball with the children, model rolling the ball, throwing the ball and kicking the ball, depending on the child's level of development.
- Hold a child's hand and jump with him/her, encourage the children to jump around on the grass.
- Encourage the children to climb stairs, holding onto their hands.
- Provide a small low slide for the children to slide down.
- Walk up and down a gently sloping mound.
- Place a small ladder on the ground and encourage the children to step into each space between the rungs.
- Provide the children with pull along toys.
- Sit in the sandpit with the children on a low seat nearby and model filling and emptying a bucket of sand. Give the children a variety of containers to fill and empty.
- Place a low table outside and give the children finger paint to use on the table; give them a small amount of paint to use.
- Give the children paint, brushes and paper. Model how to use the brushes and paint.
- Place toys on a rug on the verandah, blocks, simple construction toys, cars, trains, toy animals, people etc. Model how to use the toys, stack blocks with a child, build an enclosure for the animals. Talk about the animals, the sounds they make, make the sounds together. Make a ramp for the cars, model how to use the ramp.
- Set up a home corner, on the verandah, on a play platform, in a cubby house, or under a tree. Always provide the children with realistic props, and make sure there is always something available to encourage children's pretend play — something that the child can use to act out roles they have seen in their environment.
- Place a table and some chairs in the area, place a plastic picnic set with plates, cups and spoons, saucepans, containers, and brooms in the home corner. Act out making dinner, talk about what you are cooking, pretend to eat the dinner.
- Place some water in a baby's bath, encourage the children to bath the dolls and dry them with a towel.
- Wash the dishes that have been used in the sandpit or in the home corner.
- Involve the children with cleaning up the playground, bring out wheelbarrows, carts or buckets and tidy the playground together.
- Water the garden with small watering cans, talk about the plants.
- Sing, dance and play games in the playground, on the grass or on the verandah depending on the type of game.

Planning the outdoor play environment

To illustrate a concept design for a playground designed for the under twos, we'll use an example from a children's centre. The concept design is shown in Figure 4.2. Such a playground must cater for a wide range of needs, some of which can be in conflict. Small immobile babies require a quiet place to lie whereas the active one-year-olds enjoy the freedom to explore. The recently mobile toddler is still at the stage where everything goes into the mouth, whereas the older toddlers can explore without putting things in their mouths. The placement of the various play features and natural features must be considered carefully so that all groups using the area are catered for without placing any one group at risk.

The whole area needs to be free of trip hazards such as raised edges around sandpits, swings, lawns and soft-fall areas, as young children do not look where they are going and are already unsteady on their feet without the added the risk of tripping.

A path of non-slip pavers leads from the verandah to a storage shed in the northern corner of the playground. This path passes a large sandpit at ground level where children can enter without the risk of tripping over the edges. A sandpit at ground level also gives staff the opportunity of sweeping the overflow of sand on the surrounding paths back into the sandpit.

A bench seat on one side of the sandpit provides for a staff member to sit and nurse a baby or an upset child whilst still interacting with other children in the sandpit. The whole area is covered by very large shade sails to protect the children from the sun. A tap between the sandpit and the shed provides access to water so that the sand can be dampened. Damp sand gives children the opportunity to build mounds and dig holes successfully whereas construction is impossible with dry sand. Damp sand also reduces the amount of sand blowing onto the paths on windy days and creating a hazard.

A grassed area on the eastern side of the sandpit provides the children with a place to crawl, roll and play ball. A low, mounded area acts as a deterrent to crawling babies who may crawl unnoticed into the swing area. Young children also enjoy sitting or standing on top of a raised area.

On the north-eastern fence amongst some trees, a small play platform with steps and railing provides children with the opportunity to climb a couple of steps, observe other children in the playground from a slightly elevated position and to play house if and when furniture and props have been placed in the structure.

On the southern side of the playground there is a double swing area with low bench seats either side for staff and children to sit on. These seats also act as a deterrent to children who may wander into the area. Babies need swing seats with sides, a back and a fastening front that secures them as they swing, toddlers can be placed in a tyre basket swing attachment.

The soft-fall under the swings is wood chips as it is situated far enough away from the babies who are likely to put the chips in their

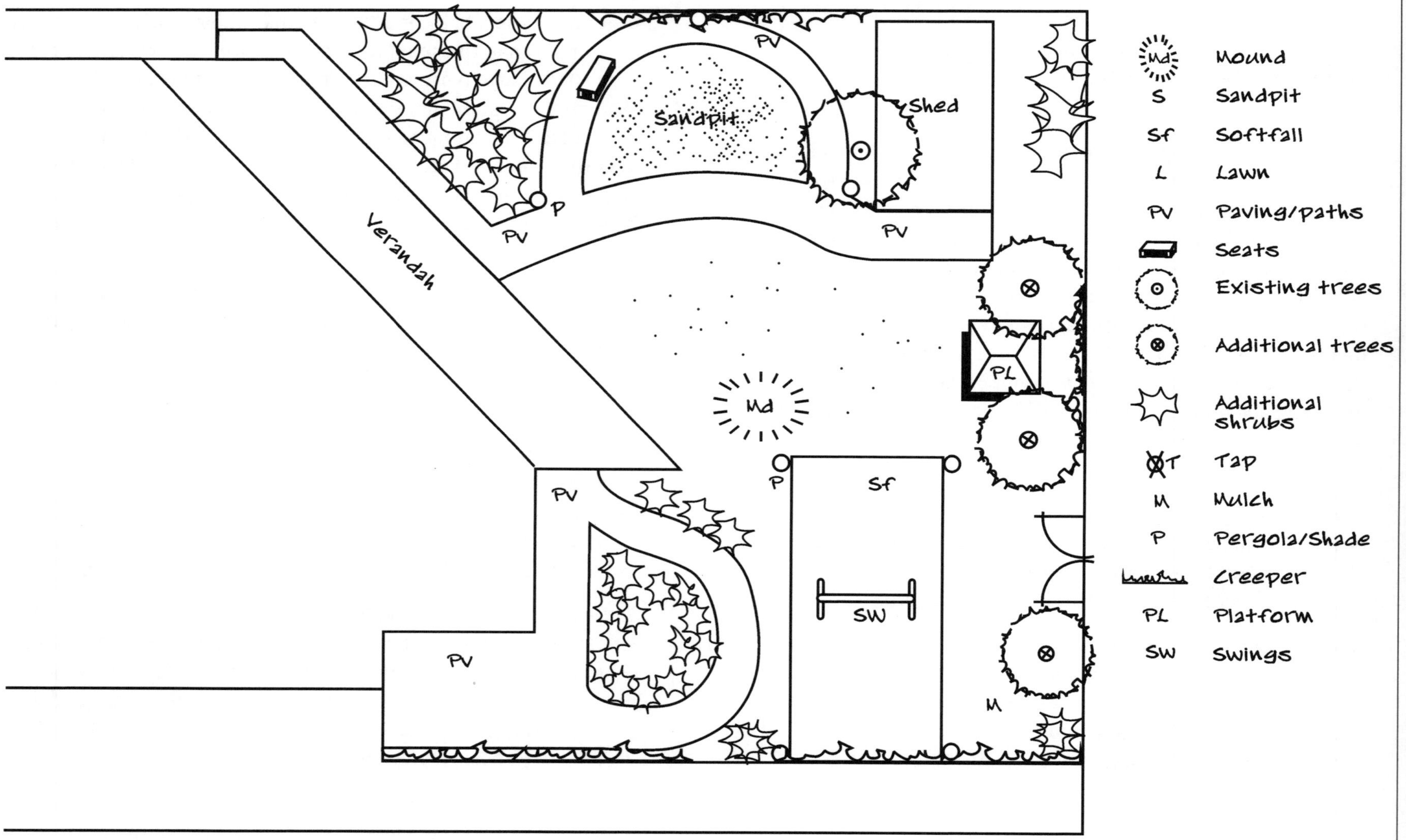

Figure 4.2 Concept design for Children's Centre playground

mouth. However, a rubberised surface although expensive, would be safer and preferable in a playground for under twos. The soft-fall area under the swings can also be used for movable climbing frames when the swings are not set up. The area between the swings and the eastern fence has a garden where daisies and other flowering plants grow. This area is a place for children to explore, wander among the plants and smell the flowers.

A winding track around a garden area provides children with a place to use push–pull toys and ride-on wheeled toys. Access to this track is from the verandah as well as from the lawn area.

chapter 5 Outdoor areas for children aged two to three-and-a-half years

There is a broad range of developmental levels in this age group and it is of vital importance that the individual needs of all the children are met.

Some early childhood centres have three play areas, one for the under twos, another for the two- to three-year-olds and the other for the three- to five-year-old children, but most have only two, one for the under twos and the other for the over twos.

When two-year-olds move from the babies' section to the over twos' section and have to play alongside older children they can be at risk of being overwhelmed by more boisterous play where the play features are not always appropriate for them and they seem to get lost in the crowd. They are attracted to the more interesting type of play of the older children, but when they try to join in they lack the skills and often disrupt play, resulting in conflict and unhappiness. It is important in these situations that staff make an effort to separate these younger children and give them some time in the playground when the older children are inside.

It is appropriate to bring all the groups together at some time during the day as it provides a family grouping where older children can be encouraged to consider the younger ones, and the younger ones can benefit from interactions with the older children.

Grouping by age is only an approximation of what children might be expected to do, a wider age range can cater for those children more or less advanced in particular developmental areas as they will have the opportunity to interact with children at their same developmental level. Mixed age grouping can be beneficial all round, particularly in the area of socialisation, but each age group does need time to work and play with peers.

If a playground is to cater for all children over two years, it is useful to have two sandpits, or a two-sectioned sandpit where the younger children can play away from the more boisterous children. In order to cater for all the age groups using a playground, swing frames with pigtail hooks that allow for different types of swings to be attached need to be installed. Age-appropriate climbing can be provided as low, flexible, fixed structures allow for movable equipment such as boards and ladders to be attached. It all depends, however, on the amount of space available. (See Chapter 2 for a discussion on shared space.)

The developmental stages listed in this chapter have been chosen specifically for their suitability to be fostered by outdoor experiences.

Children (24–30 months)

Gross motor development

Table 5.1 lists some of the physical skills children begin to develop at this age.

TABLE 5.1 GROSS MOTOR DEVELOPMENT

Children (24–30 months):

- Engage in a great deal of physical play
- Can walk up and down one step, and progress to walking up stairs
- Can jump with two feet
- Enjoy climbing into large cardboard boxes
- Enjoy sitting on wheeled toys that they can steer and push with their feet
- Can roll a ball, kick a ball, throw a large ball
- Enjoy being pushed gently on a swing, rolling down small slopes and the feel of sliding down a short slide

This age group needs a soft grassy area with plenty of space where they can run, jump, climb and play ball. Many of them may still be unsteady on their feet, experimenting with their jumping and climbing and having numerous falls as they practise their skills. All these activities will need an adult nearby to guide the children and help maintain their interest and assist the development of their large motor skills.

A sturdy portable piece of age-appropriate climbing equipment, which includes a slide, could be placed on the lawn from time to time when the space is not needed for other activities. It is important to leave plenty of space around the different activities placed on the lawn so that children can move safely between activities and nothing is hidden from their view, as they only use what they can see.

The children will also need a hard-surfaced path where they can push their ride-on wheeled toys, prams, wheelbarrows and carts. A path with wide gentle corners is a good idea so they can learn to negotiate the bends without too many problems.

A small mound approx 250 mm high with several steps up on one side and with the other side gradually sloping down will provide the children with the opportunity to climb up and jump down safely, or roll down. Rolling down a slope or along the ground requires whole body coordination and requires practice to perfect this skill.

A double swing frame could be placed in the playground. The gentle movement of a swing is very soothing to young children and with a soft basket-tyre swing attachment, the children will have a feeling of security. A double swing frame is preferable to a single one as it gives the children the opportunity to swing alongside another child.

Impact-absorbing material must be placed underneath the swing area to the depth recommended by the Australian Standards or by your local licensing body. Only use materials that have been tested for impact absorption and ensure they are at the appropriate depth.

Fine motor development

Table 5.2 lists skills children in this age group need to develop to strengthen the muscles in their hands and fingers.

TABLE 5.2 FINE MOTOR DEVELOPMENT

Children (24–30 months):

- Are able to manipulate small objects such as cars, and small dolls
- Like to put small objects into small spaces and fit lids on containers
- Enjoy exploring materials and textures
- Love to play with sand and water.
- Will pile and stack blocks, particularly if modelled first by an adult
- Will use large crayons, paints and brushes

The children will need an area where they can use simple construction toys and blocks, a place for miniature cars and trucks, a place to dance to music and where staff can roll out a carpet square or a rug. A section of a verandah is ideal as staff can monitor the use of the small toys and children feel comfortable being close to the building. This is an age where children prefer to be reasonably close to an adult.

Another area that provides children with the opportunity to play with small objects is the sandpit. The sandpit should be large enough for children to push cars and trucks through the sand, fill buckets and containers, use spades, and scoops and construct simple sand castles with help from caring adults. If the sand is damp, children can dig, mould and construct. Wet sand offers some resistance and requires the children to use pressure as they construct, which develops the muscles in the fingers.

Always ensure that all the containers are emptied of water before staff leave the area.

Water play can be provided in a container in the sand or in a separate water trough with jugs for pouring, funnels, water wheels, colanders and containers.

It is useful to have some tables and chairs on a verandah or in a shady area where children can sit and draw, use finger paints or any other tabletop activity appropriate to their needs.

Social and emotional development

Table 5.3 outlines some areas of development for this age group.

TABLE 5.3 SOCIAL AND EMOTIONAL DEVELOPMENT

Children (24–30 months):

- Like to play near other children, watching them and maybe playing alongside them
- Like to dress-up and begin by putting on simple garments such as caps or slippers
- Begin pretend play using familiar objects such as dolls, teddies, blocks, balls, wheeled toys, and domestic objects in their play
- Are becoming extremely independent and this can create problems for staff and peers in that they take risks, and try things they are not safely able to do
- Do have difficulty sharing, and tend to store possessions away from the others
- Become easily frustrated
- Some have difficulties separating

At two children are becoming more interested in their peers. They are fascinated by what others are doing and often want to play alongside, copying their actions. Therefore it is important to have more than one of the toys they most like to use, such as dolls, puppets, cars, brooms, tricycles, buckets and spades etc., so that they can join in the play with minimum frustration.

More use will be made of the bike track at this age with children spending long periods of time on the bikes. Keeping to the track may be a problem as they often like to take the tricycle with them when they move to the next activity that appeals.

A flat place, preferably lawn, would provide the opportunity for children to explore large cardboard boxes, and provide a place for a small table, chairs and a picnic set for pretend play. Most of the pretend play will be short in duration and tend to be of a roving kind where children engage in pretend play that imitates roles they have seen in their everyday life.

A cubbyhouse can be very restrictive in that the size dictates the number of children who can use it at any one time. However, it could be useful for this age group as they only play alongside one another or fleetingly with another child. It would need to have furniture and a few props in it at all times for it to be used. A bush cubby, a play platform or a corner on a verandah would be just as useful and would provide more space.

It is important to have a wide range of activities that do not have a right or wrong way of use. Activities such as sand and water play and props for pretend play will cater for the wide range of abilities and still allow children with different skills to play in the same area.

It is most important that the play area is safe and secure as these children are fiercely independent and if they are having trouble separating with a parent or caregiver, they may decide to go home.

Cognitive development

Table 5.4 lists some of the developments in children's thinking skills enabling them to make better sense of their environment.

TABLE 5.4 COGNITIVE DEVELOPMENT

Children at 24–30 months:

- Enjoy using simple musical instruments
- Enjoy dancing to music, moving legs, arms or body in response to music, unaware of keeping in time to the beat of the music
- Can match sounds to familiar things
- Like to help pack away and know where familiar things are kept
- Are very interested in textures
- Enjoy sand and water
- Are interested in birds, leaves, flowers, animals

Access to a tape recorder or CD player would be useful as it would give staff the opportunity to provide music for the children to move to. Spontaneous use of simple musical instruments and dancing to music on the verandah would provide the children with different sounds and develop their interest in music.

As children are becoming aware of where toys are kept and are interested in helping an adult pack things away, containers for outside toys need to be placed near activities so that children can be involved in the packing-up process.

These children still rely on their senses to help them explore and understand the world around them, therefore the playground needs to be rich in sensory experiences. A variety of paths of different textures leading children to a bush cubby, the sandpit or any other area of interest will give them the opportunity to explore the different surfaces under foot, the soft spongy feel of mulch or sawdust, the hard feel and sound of their feet on the cement or pavers. Children love the feel of dry and wet sand on their hands and feet, so make sure there is always some part of the sandpit that is dry and another wet.

Include an exploratory area in the playground where children, with the help of staff, can look for ladybirds, snails and worms, water plants with small watering cans and pick flowers.

Suggestions for staff

Table 5.5 provides staff with some ideas to facilitate children's learning.

TABLE 5.5 SUGGESTIONS FOR STAFF WORKING WITH CHILDREN 24–30 MONTHS
• Create a cosy area either on the verandah or under a shady tree with soft cushions and read stories, or look at pictures with two or three children.
• Talk to them about the pictures. Choose books about outdoors, help them link the story with the real object.
• Do not expect children at this age to stay long in one place, as their concentration may not allow it and often they are physically unable to sit in one place for any length of time.
• Set up large pillows on the grass that children can climb over.
• Play ball games with the children, encourage them to run and chase a ball and run up and down low mounds.
• Encourage the children to walk up and down steps, hold their hands if they are unsteady or nervous.
• Place a wide board on the grass for children to walk along.
• Set up a baby bath on a low table with dolls to wash and sponges to squeeze.
• Set up a table with finger paint, encourage children to move their fingers and hands around in the paint. Demonstrate the actions. This activity is good for the release of tension. Both adults and children are more relaxed when actively involved.
• Place a rug or carpet square on the verandah with a box of blocks for stacking nearby, stack a few blocks in front of the children just to give them an idea of how to use them.
• Set up the sandpit with buckets and spades, dig with the children in the sand, introduce water into the sand.
• Walk around the garden with the children, talk about the flowers, feel the leaves, listen to the sounds of the leaves rustling in the trees, the birds and any other sound that the children might recognise.
• Set an area with a table and chairs, brooms, telephone, hats and bags or a plastic picnic set, but do not put too many things out at once for this age group.
• If the children do not seem to know how to use the area, model talking on the phone or sweeping the floor, then find a reason why the child needs to take over, for example, they are wanted on the phone.

Children (30–36 months)

Children's development varies greatly in all areas and some children will be more advanced in one area than another.

Gross motor development

Table 5.6 shows an increase in gross motor skills in the last six months.

TABLE 5.6 GROSS MOTOR DEVELOPMENT

Children at 30–36 months:
• Climb, run, and jump
• Can throw and kick a large ball
• Walk up and down steps using alternate feet
• Walk on tip-toes
• Jump down from a low step
• Are beginning to use pedals on a tricycle and can balance on one foot for a short time

For the children to develop the large muscles in their arms and legs they need a large area, preferably grass where they can run, jump, roll, and play ball. The grassy area provides space to place a box to throw bean bags into, a place to lay out a rope to jump over and a place to lie a ladder flat on the ground for children to walk into each space between the rungs.

An undulating surface or even a mound if the area can support one would provide children with safe climbing. A mound with a path and steps up and gently sloping sides is less likely to be eroded. Many mounds are placed in playgrounds where there is not really enough room and the result is a high mound with steep sides that are eroded by children climbing and sliding down the sides.

The wear and tear of children's feet should not be underestimated. If the play area is small then it is more appropriate to have a piece of climbing equipment that is age-appropriate with soft-fall to Australian Standards (see Chapter 1) under and around the structure. Make sure that the equipment is going to provide the children with the activities they need at this stage and that it does not duplicate an experience already present in the playground.

This age group will still use a bike track but it can double as an exploratory area when bikes are not in use. Edge the track with trees and plants that provide different perfumes, colour and textures.

Fine motor development

Table 5.7 lists some of the fine motor skills children of this age will develop.

TABLE 5.7 FINE MOTOR DEVELOPMENT

Children at 30–36 months:

- Can pour liquid from a jug into a container
- Can open and close scissors, but are unable to cut successfully
- Enjoy finger painting using whole hand
- Like to fit lids on small containers
- Can handle delicate things with adult support
- Enjoy sand and water play
- Can stack blocks

Many fine motor activities can be provided in the outdoors. The sandpit with access to water will give the children the opportunity to pour, empty and fill containers, and fit lids on containers. Digging in the sand by hand will further develop and strengthen the finger and hand muscles. Buckets and spades and other sand toys also need to be provided.

Ensure that all containers of water are emptied out and all running water is turned off before leaving the area.

The provision of tabletop activities either under the verandah, in a sheltered paved area or even on grass will give the children the opportunity to experiment with finger paint, paste, hold scissors and attempt to cut. The most important aspect of these activities is to make sure that there is not the expectation from staff or parents of an end product as the experimenting and exploring are the most important aspects at this stage.

Picking flowers, picking up leaves and handling a ladybird or a snail with adult support will encourage the children to respect and appreciate nature and learn how to handle precious objects.

Social and emotional development

Table 5.8 shows the development of social skills, in that children of this age are beginning to play with other children.

TABLE 5.8 SOCIAL AND EMOTIONAL DEVELOPMENT

Children at 30–36 months:

- Engage in pretend play
- Enjoy pretend play of familiar roles, simple pretend play — putting babies to bed, and talking on the telephone
- Begin to play with other children

- Will dress up with hats, bags and shoes
- Enjoy small group activities
- Are beginning to share
- Begin to express feelings
- Become more aware of other children and how they feel
- Have increasing independence

Figure 5.1 These children are acting out the role of parents complete with baby, bags and pushers

Pretend play or dramatic play as it is often called is very important to children's development. It is through dramatic play or socio-dramatic play where they play a pretend game with another child that they use language, solve problems and learn to communicate and cooperate with other children.

There needs to be a wide range of materials available to these children for their pretend play. They will dress-up with another child, push their dolls in pushers around the bike track with another child, ride their trikes with another child to go to 'the shops'. All themes that are very familiar to all children and are part of their life (see Figure 5.1).

Cognitive development

The cognitive development stages listed in Table 5.9 can be fostered by outdoor experiences.

TABLE 5.9 COGNITIVE DEVELOPMENT

Children at 30–36 months:

- Enjoy exploring their environment
- Remember and follow simple rules
- Are beginning to know same and different
- Know and stay away from dangers when reminded

- Help tell a story
- Dance to music
- Enjoy digging in the sand
- Can assemble a simple jigsaw
- Construct simple block structures
- Are beginning to sort colours with adult support and modelling
- Are beginning to use objects to represent things, ie block of wood for a car

As their pretend play becomes more developed, they are able to use one object to represent another, for example, using a piece of wood for a telephone, symbolic play begins to emerge. Props for this kind of play need to be provided both indoors and outdoors.

Belinda uses a garden hose to represent a hose on a petrol pump:

● Belinda (34 months) sitting on a ride-on toy motor bike, pushed with her feet so that the motor bike moved along the path. She reached the verandah post where a garden hose was looped around a wheel with the nozzle of the hose hanging down. She pulled the hose towards the back of her motor bike, placed the nozzle so that it touched the back wheel for a short time then dropped the hose and continued down the path pushing the motor bike along the path towards the sandpit. ●

Construction play also develops — block play of stacking blocks and building simple bridges can extend to the building of enclosures. A flat area, such as a verandah or paved area with a carpet square or some indoor/outdoor carpet, will provide space for this activity. Collections of plastic animals, people or cars would encourage this type of play. This area would also be useful for simple sorting activities.

Small baskets, wheelbarrows and buckets are useful containers for children to collect and sort different flowers, leaves and any other natural materials in the outdoors.

If a tree drops leaves in autumn or seeds or pine cones, do not be in a hurry to clean them up. Apart from the collecting and sorting, dry autumn leaves make a wonderful sound when children walk through them.

Children need a grassed area where they can engage in simple circle games or musical games with guidance from an adult or dance spontaneously to music. Taped music gives the children a chance to move to the music and simple musical instruments that they can shake, rattle or bang enrich their musical experiences.

Suggestions for staff

Table 5.10 provides staff with some ideas to facilitate children's learning.

TABLE 5.10 SUGGESTIONS FOR STAFF WORKING WITH CHILDREN 30–36 MONTHS

- Encourage children to throw bean bags or a ball at or into a box.
- Provide them with large boxes that they can climb in and out of.
- Give them pegs to use to hang up paintings, dolls clothes etc as this will strengthen the muscles in their fingers, even pegs around a plastic ice cream tin could be presented as a game to play.
- Encourage the children to make balls and 'snakes' at the dough or clay table. The adult may need to model first. This activity is for children to become familiar with the medium, to exercise the muscles in the fingers and hands, and to have fun. The important part for the child is the doing not the end product.
- Provide the children with water in a trough or baby bath and give them jugs and containers to pour, fill and empty.
- Introduce the children to sorting activities by asking them to pick up 'all the big blocks' at packing up time or any other suitable object and putting them away. This way you are combining an activity with a packing-up time task.
- Involve the children in a gardening activity. Planting seeds or seedlings, watering the plants with small watering cans. Make sure there are enough watering cans for those interested in helping.
- Introduce visiting pets that the children feed, or nurse with adult supervision.
- Provide the children with easy to wear dress-ups. Men's shirts with the sleeves shortened or rolled up, jackets, short nightdresses — clothes that are loose-fitting, go on over the head or with large buttons or zips.
- Set up a 'home corner' area.
- Ensure that you are providing culturally inclusive materials in your day-to-day work with the children.

Empty water from containers before leaving the area.

Children (36–42 months)

Gross motor development

The developmental stages in Table 5.11 have been included for their suitability to be fostered by outdoor play.

TABLE 5.11 GROSS MOTOR DEVELOPMENT

Children at 36–42 months:
• Walk up and down stairs using alternate feet
• Can run, jump and hop
• Walk on tiptoes
• Enjoy rough and tumble play
• Balance on one foot for a very short time
• Walk along a wide board on the ground
• Can ride a bike, beginning to use the pedals
• Catch, kick and throw a large ball
• Enjoy climbing
• Will use a small slide
• Can balance on one foot

If the play area is large enough, place a long, low, undulating mound either to one side or near the back of the play area. Place some steps up to the top and put a small slide into the mound. A path of compacted building sand, garden mulch or sawdust could wind from the top of the steps to the slide and along the top of the mound and down. A few perfumed plants could be planted along one side of the path.

If there is not enough room for a mound, a simple age-appropriate climbing structure with a slide and steps could be placed in soft-fall.

Make sure that there is an area of grass where the children can practise walking along a wide board on the ground, doing somersaults, jumping and hopping, throwing and kicking balls and generally engaging in rough and tumble games.

A paved path for trikes to one side or at the back of the playground provides the children with the opportunity to practise their riding as some of them will be at the stage where they can negotiate the pedals. It is always a good idea to incorporate some area suitable for pretend play nearby so that the riding of tricycles can extend into pretend play.

Fine motor development

The developmental stages listed in Table 5.12 show an increase in children's fine motor skills in the past six months.

TABLE 5.12 FINE MOTOR DEVELOPMENT

Children at 36–42 months:
• Hand and finger muscles are strengthening
• Can pick up small things with pincer grip (finger and thumb)
• Are beginning to do up buttons and zips

- Fit lids on jars
- Pour from a small jug into a container
- Hold pencil in fingers
- Enjoy finger paint using the whole hand and fingers
- Enjoy clay and dough
- Are beginning to use scissors with adult help
- Enjoy pasting materials on paper
- Enjoy sand and water

Some of the activities that strengthen hand and finger muscles include digging in wet sand with the hands, working with clay, squeezing sponges in water, and finger painting. A flat paved area or a verandah that is suitable for tabletop play will be needed for working with clay, using pencils, pasting and cutting with scissors. Finger painting really needs to be on a low table over a flat piece of grass so that the children have the freedom to use plenty of finger paint and the table can be hosed down.

Water in the sandpit is a must. Dry sand offers no resistance — it is the resistance that helps strengthen the finger and hand muscles. Also it is impossible to construct sand castles or roads for cars or dig holes if the sand is dry.

Children of this age enjoy dressing-up and they need a range of dress-ups with a variety of fasteners so that they can practise their newly acquired skills. Items of clothing that need to be done up are more likely to appeal to young children than using a board that has a variety of fasteners attached to it.

Social and emotional development

The developmental areas listed in Table 5.13 can be fostered by outdoor experiences.

TABLE 5.13 SOCIAL AND EMOTIONAL DEVELOPMENT

Children at 36–42 months:

- Will engage in simple socio-dramatic play for a short time, will copy adult actions such as sweeping the floor
- Put on and take off simple dress-ups
- Play easy circle games with adult support
- Use language in play with others
- Are beginning to take turns with adult support and encouragement
- Express feelings and recognise others' feelings
- Are becoming more cooperative
- Need adult help to overcome problems, social and emotional

Children need a place that can be set up with furniture and props to encourage them to engage in pretend play. A bush cubby with space for dolls' beds, tables and chairs or a small play platform that can be set up as a hospital, a shop, or a bus would also encourage pretend play as they are all situations most children are familiar with. Staff may need to model sweeping a floor, putting a doll to bed, or washing dishes to help the children in their play.

A range of props and dress-up that are not gender-specific and that introduce children to other cultures would be most appropriate.

A grassy area for simple circle games gives children the opportunity to sit on the grass, run, or crawl and it will soften any accidental fall during a running game.

Some children at this age will still prefer to play alongside other children rather than with children, and others may want to play alone. All children have a time when they need to be alone or with one other child and space needs to be available where this can happen. Small cosy corners in the playground where one or two children can withdraw from the more boisterous play of their peers must be provided. It could be in the form of a bush cubby, a tree trunk seat under a tree, or tree trunk seats in a quiet corner of the playground.

Cognitive development

Table 5.14 reveals children's curiosity and interest in the outdoors at this age.

TABLE 5.14 COGNITIVE DEVELOPMENT

Children at 36–42 months:

- Enjoy and join in with simple songs
- Can identify and match familiar objects and creatures to the sounds they make
- Paste
- Sing songs and do finger plays
- Are beginning to identify colours
- Sort colour and shapes when shown how
- Are interested in insects, birds, animals, the way they move, what they eat
- Are interested in plants and planting
- Are interested in shadows
- Enjoy sand and water play
- Explore using their senses of touch, sight, smell, taste, and hearing
- Can match objects of similar textures

An exploratory area or track where children can discover slaters, snails and worms will provide children with the opportunity to observe different types of creatures.

The playground needs to have plants with different shaped and textured leaves, different coloured flowers, different perfumes, and a herb garden with a variety of herbs that the children can taste or that can be used in cooking. There needs to be a children's garden where children can plant quick-growing flowers or vegetables with the help of staff, and water those plants with small watering cans.

Bird feeders in a nearby tree or on a stand in the garden will encourage birds into the playground, children could place food in the feeders from time to time. Wind chimes in the trees also provide different sounds for the children to identify.

A large sandpit with damp sand provides children with the opportunity to solve problems with their constructions, as well as the social problem of sharing space with another child — problems where they need to consider and respect other children and their work.

Suggestions for staff

Table 5.15 provides staff with some ideas to facilitate children's learning.

TABLE 5.15 SUGGESTIONS FOR STAFF WORKING WITH CHILDREN 36–42 MONTHS
• Have a box of different sized balls readily available that children can play with. Join in with the children kicking and throwing balls.
• Place a collection of large boxes on the grass and encourage children to climb in and out of the boxes.
• Give the children paint and large brushes to paint the boxes.
• Give the children paste and materials that can be glued onto the boxes.
• Help children to push the pedals on their trikes, remind them to push with their feet each time the pedal comes around. Keep repeating the word 'push' when the pedal comes around.
• Set up a block area on a carpet on the verandah and encourage the children to build a tower. Model how to build a small tower, then give them time to experiment.
• Place small cars or plastic animals in the block area.
• Set up tabletop activities according to the needs and interests of the children.
• Introduce finger-painting or clay and be prepared to stay with that activity talking to the children about the texture and how to use it. Adult-made models in the clay are not appropriate but pounding and

thumping the clay or squeezing it will encourage children to do the same, which will help strengthen the finger and hand muscles.

- Involve the children in the cleaning up of the clay and finger painting activities. Provide them with buckets of water and sponges and accept their efforts. Encourage them to make the table clean. Stay with them while they are cleaning up.
- Set up a cosy corner with large cushions or a table and chairs in the playground or on the verandah and read stories to the children about familiar animals, birds and insects found in the outdoors. Make sure the stories are short and the group small. Be prepared to read to one child whenever the interest is there. Have books in the area that children can look at by themselves.
- Have a felt board in the cosy corner with pictures of familiar creatures for children to play with. Talk to the children about those creatures.
- Set up a pretend play area either on a play platform, in a bush cubby or on a verandah with a carpet square on the floor. Furnish the area with a table and chairs, plastic plates, cups and saucers, dolls and dolls beds and easy to put on dress-ups. Do not put out too many items at once as the children will be overwhelmed and not use the items appropriately.
- Remember to include dress-ups that are suitable for both boys and girls and include clothing from other cultures. Staff will need to talk to the children about the different types of clothing or cooking utensils. If you have children in your centre from other cultures, involve the families in the setting-up of the home corner.
- Place several telephones in the pretend play area where children can talk on the phone to one another.

Empty the buckets before leaving the area.

- Place a tape recorder on the verandah out of the reach of children and play tapes that children can move to spontaneously. Staff may need to join in to involve children who seem interested but unsure of what to do.
- Have a range of sand toys that can be changed from time to time. Place a box of toys at the side of the sandpit ready for the children to use. Pack away at the end of each outdoor playtime and involve the children in the packing-up. A sandpit full of toys left in the sandpit from the previous playtime does not have the appeal that an empty sandpit with a basket full of toys nearby has for children, they do not like other children's 'left-overs'.

Planning the outdoor play environment

For children aged two to three-and-a-half the area needs to be large enough for all the children to have space to play without the feeling of being crowded. Too many children of this age in a small space tends to lead to fights. It must be remembered that these children are still learning to share space, toys, and staff attention.

It is also important that the area is not cluttered with too many structures but has enough space around any structures as well as space for movable equipment and toys that can be used in a variety of situations, such as in the sand, on a mat on the verandah or in pretend play. Children of this age have a preference for small toys particularly those that can be used in the sand — an extremely popular play material.

These children are becoming more independent but still rely on adult support, encouragement or presence in most situations. It is important therefore that there are seats available for staff in a variety of settings throughout the playground — seats where they can interact with other children while comforting an upset child, a place where they can support and encourage children in their explorations and discoveries or a place where they can observe children's play behaviours without being actively involved.

To illustrate a concept design we'll use an example from a playground designed for children between the ages of six weeks and three years (see the concept design in Figure 5.2). It is important for readers to be aware that this plan was designed to cater for the needs of one particular centre and would not necessarily be suitable for other locations.

This centre gained approval to extend their care program to include children under two years old. They acquired more land and decided to redevelop their existing playgrounds. Although the building had a separate section for the children under two, the decision was made to have one playground to cater for all children under three years of age.

In the north-eastern corner a swing area suitable for only very young children has been erected with a recycled rubber surface underneath to ensure that there are no small particles babies and toddlers can put in their mouths. A shade port stands over the swing area.

A quiet area nearby is designed so that staff can sit and nurse young babies or interact with them as they crawl on the lawn. This area is also a place where children can withdraw from the noise and boisterous play in the rest of the playground

A low, grassed mound in the quiet area, approximately 100 mm high, gently sloping, more undulating than mounded, provides a place where young children can climb, roll and stand on top.

A well-established tree near the verandah provides shade to a large part of the playground and a seat around the tree gives staff and children the opportunity to sit and watch children at play.

A small sandpit under the verandah provides opportunities for babies to play in the sand away from the more boisterous children. This sandpit was part of the original playground but was too small to cater for the number of children using the playground.

A winding track of non-slip pavers provides a place for children to use push–pull toys and ride-on wheeled toys. Inside this path herbs have been planted and outside hardy flowering plants have been planted. This track has been positioned so that the push–pull toys do not intrude on areas where children are engaged in quiet play or where children are likely to be running, thus reducing the likelihood of collisions. It also acts as a barrier between the more active and the quiet areas.

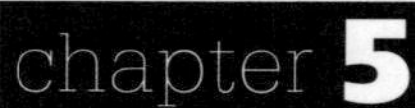

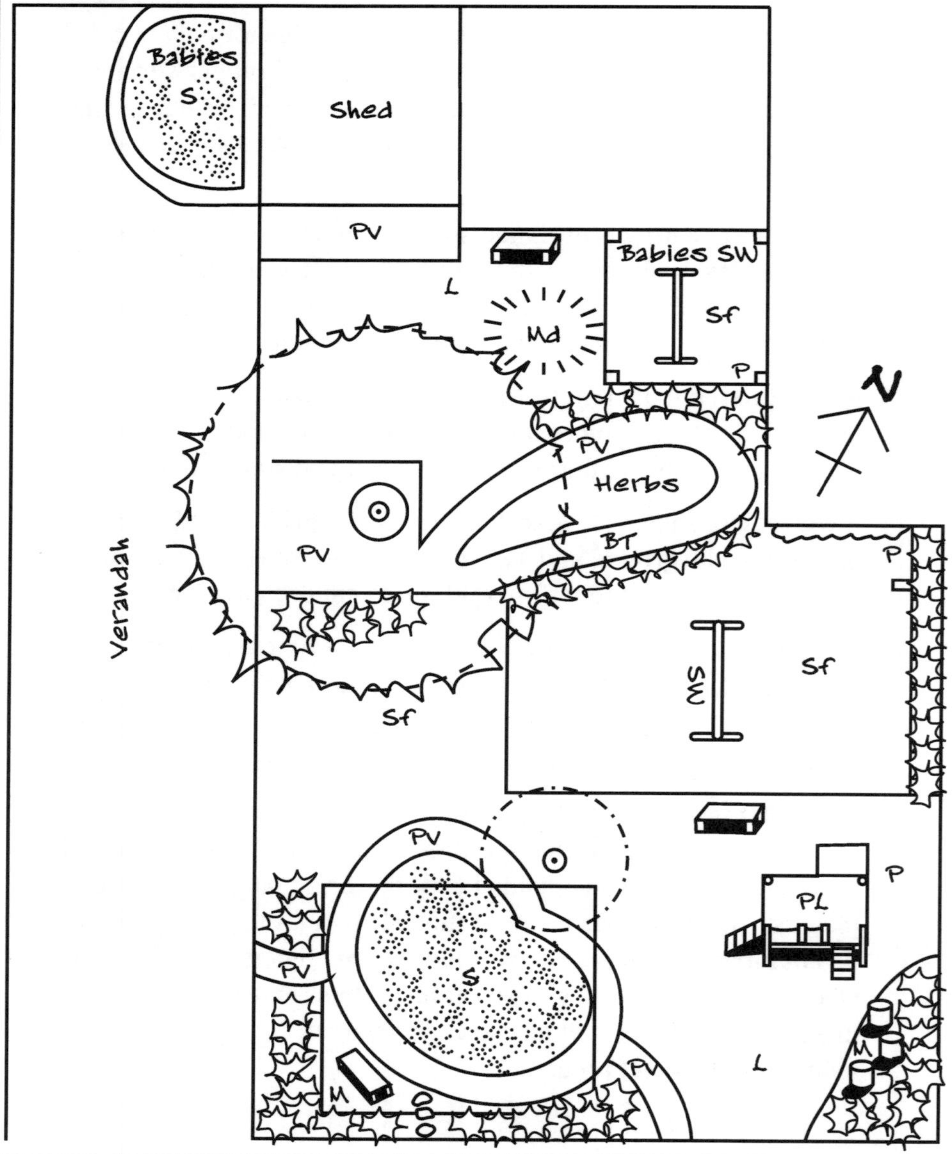
Babies S
Shed
PV
Babies SW
Sf
L
Md
P
PV
Herbs
BT
PV
P
Verandah
SW
Sf
Sf
PV
P
PL
PV
S
M
PV
L
M
N

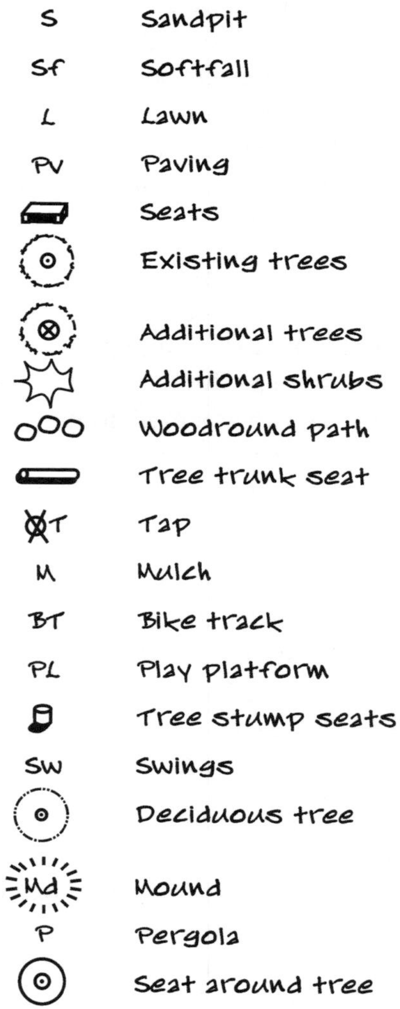
S Sandpit
Sf Softfall
L Lawn
PV Paving
Seats
Existing trees
Additional trees
Additional shrubs
Woodround path
Tree trunk seat
T Tap
M Mulch
BT Bike track
PL Play platform
Tree stump seats
SW Swings
Deciduous tree
Md Mound
P Pergola
Seat around tree

Figure 5.2 Concept design of a playground for children six weeks to three years

On the eastern fence a double swing frame with pigtail hooks gives staff the opportunity to change the swing attachments according to the children's needs. The toddlers can be placed in a tyre basket swing attachment. Soft-fall under this swing is wood chips.

In the south-western corner a large sandpit at ground level with a pergola covered in shade cloth provides children with the opportunity to dig, construct, and generally explore the medium. A tap is provided so that children can have buckets of water to mix and stir. Damp sand is essential in the summer to reduce the possibility of sand blowing into the children's eyes and onto paths rendering them slippery and a hazard. All around the edge a path of non-slip pavers approximately 300 mm wide allows for sand to be swept back into the sandpit.

A seat in the corner of the sandpit allows staff to sit and interact with the children as they play. A paved path links the sandpit with the two verandahs as the wear and tear to and from the sandpit would destroy any grassed area. All around the south-western sides medium-sized plants provide shelter and cosiness.

In the middle of the lawn a small play platform 200 mm high with safety fencing and steps up one side and a ramp up the other provides a place for children to experience what it is like to be up 'high', a place to sit at a table and chairs using a telephone or a place for dolls beds and dolls to encourage the children's pretend play. This particular centre covered the timber floor, steps and ramp with outdoor carpet to soften any falls.

Throughout the playground small gardens of hardy plants such as daisies, rosemary and a variety of geraniums provide colour, flowers to smell and pick, places to sit. Tree stump seats in mulch also provide low seating for children.

chapter 6 Outdoor areas for children aged three-and-a-half to five years

The needs, interests and skills of the children in this age range vary considerably depending on their different life experiences, gender and cultural norms. The amount of previous adult support they've had can affect their development. Children coming from homes where the family is interested in nature and outdoor activities are more likely to have an interest in these areas. Some families will have supported children's socio-dramatic play to the point where they are proficient players.

Gender differences, particularly in the gross motor and fine motor developmental areas, become apparent with boys tending to be more advanced in gross motor skills requiring power, such as running and jumping, whereas girls appear more developed in fine motor skills and gross motor skills that require coordination of the whole body, skills required in rolling, skipping and swinging (Berry 1993; Berk 1996).

Staff who work with Indigenous Australian children have noticed that the children in this age group are more skillful in gross motor activities than the non-Aboriginal children. All these differences need to be taken into consideration when planning an outdoor program for this age group.

Although developmental areas have been introduced separately in this chapter it is important to remember that all the activities and experiences provided for children facilitate growth in many developmental areas at the same time. The developmental indicators for the three-and-a-half-year old children and the four- to five-year-old children have been presented together before the descriptions of the environments supporting those areas. As mentioned above, children in this age range vary greatly in their development and some will be more advanced in one area than in another; for example, they may be physically more advanced but emotionally and socially operating at a younger level. The play environment needs to be similar, but the way the children use it will differ depending on their level of development.

Many playground designs in the past have catered mainly for the physical development of children ignoring the importance of their social, emotional and cognitive developmental needs. Therefore it is very important that decision-makers are made aware of all the developmental needs of children and that the outdoors provides a very valuable learning environment.

We need to foster the learning and intellectual development of all children by providing long periods of uninterrupted time and space for sustained play where they can learn about their environment. They need a range of experiences that will allow them to explore, observe, problem-solve, question and make discoveries that will increase their understanding of the world around them and the effects they can have on their environment. As the senses still play a major role in this age group's learning, they need to have a variety of activities and experiences involving the senses. They need activities that give them the opportunity to interact with others developing language and social skills.

Socio-dramatic play fosters both language and social skills. As Creaser (1990b, p. 12) says:

> Language of pretend play gains in complexity as the social scene develops and more children become involved. Social competence is challenged … Children together learn to solve problems, negotiate roles and positions.

Gross motor development

Outdoor play areas should be designed to encourage children to move from one area of interest to another over a period of time, using and experiencing all that the outdoors can offer. The more interesting the outdoors the more children will explore and discover.

The skills of children in this age group vary considerably, as is evident in Table 6.1.

TABLE 6.1 GROSS MOTOR DEVELOPMENT

Children at 42–48 months can:

- hop on one foot
- balance on one foot for a few seconds
- walk heel to toe
- begin to gallop
- jump off a step
- jump over objects
- catch a large ball
- carry heavier things
- begin to do forward somersaults
- steer and pedal a tricycle
- use a slide without help
- begin to pump a swing

Children at 48–60 months can:

- run with ease
- run and kick a ball
- hit a large ball with a large bat
- catch a bounced ball

- throw a small ball at a target
- pump up a swing and maintain its momentum
- climb up and down ladders with alternate feet

Children need space to run, jump, and play ball games. If the centre does not have sufficient space for these types of activities, it is most important that staff find a nearby oval, park or school grounds where these activities can be provided from time to time. Grassed areas are the most suitable for running, and doing somersaults, hard surfaces are useful for bouncing balls.

The most useful types of climbing equipment for this age group are those that are flexible and can be changed according to the needs and interests of the children. Movable boards and ladders are useful as they can be added to certain structures designed for attachments (see Chapter 1). Equipment that can be changed and added to ensures that children will always find it interesting, whereas static equipment becomes uninteresting and rarely used once the novelty wears off.

The positioning of swings is important as children use swings as a watching place. They watch other children at play from the safety of a swing and move from the swing to other activities and areas of interest once they have 'checked it out'.

Climbing equipment, slides and swings all need quite a large area and construction and positioning must conform to safety regulations. The most important safety aspect is the type and depth of impact-absorbent material underneath equipment that will ensure the risk to children is reduced should they fall.

Swings should never be positioned in the middle of the play area as children will unthinkingly run through the area often colliding with a swinging child. It is preferable that one side or back of the swing area is on a fence line. Narrow garden beds with hardy flowering plants such as daisies on either side of the swing area will deter children from running in from the side, or low bench seats where children can sit and talk to friends as they swing or wait for a turn will act as barriers to the running child.

An alternative to a climbing structure is a long gently sloping mound that can include some of the features of climbing equipment with less risk. These mounds are only successful however if there is plenty of space. Small high steep mounds erode; children's feet continually pound and scrape away the soil and plants do not survive.

A slide can be placed into the mound with steps next to the slide for access from the base of the mound. A slide with a slow finish, so that the body is almost stationary when the child reaches the bottom, is preferable and means that there is less hollowing out at the bottom of the slide.

A clatterbridge placed between two undulations on a mound would be of interest to children. It needs to be low to the ground for safety. Access to the bridge could be a path of rolled building sand winding up from the base of the mounded area. Aesthetically paths need to be of natural materials such as garden mulch, sand or compacted sawdust as they have a more natural appearance and blend in with the surrounding plants.

A variety of steps and narrow textured paths could wind up the mound leading to an area of interest such as a sitting area or a rocky area filled with fine sand suitable for dramatic play with cars, trucks, and other toys. Planting along the edges of some of the paths will add to the feeling of adventure and exploration. Narrow winding paths are more interesting to children than wide ones and the use of paths in other areas of the playground will draw children into an area as they create a sense of mystery as to what is around the corner or over the bridge. Children need a reason to use paths; they need to lead to some area of interest.

Bike tracks are often seen as unnecessary for this age group as many of the children have bikes at home and can ride them proficiently. It does depend however on the needs of the children. All bike tracks need to be positioned at the side or back of the playground away from the busy areas otherwise they present a safety hazard with children on bikes colliding with running children. They need to have a simple section for the learners and a more challenging section with undulations, archways and rumble strips for the more proficient riders. Sensory plants either side of the track and parking stations add challenge and interest (see Chapter 1).

Fine motor development

As the strength in the hand and fingers muscles have increased, children of this age group engage happily in art and craft activities as shown in Table 6.2.

TABLE 6.2 FINE MOTOR DEVELOPMENT

Children at 42–48 months can:

- hammer nails
- do up large buttons
- pick up tiny things
- pour and fill
- pin a peg
- screw on a lid
- do inset puzzles
- build with blocks
- paint with a brush
- hold a pencil with fingers
- manipulate dough and clay

Children at 48–60 months can:

- cut on a line with scissors
- print a few known letters
- enjoy jigsaws
- fold paper
- use dough and clay to create

- have a mature grasp of a pencil or brush
- paint recognisable paintings with a brush
- pour water into a small container
- build complex block structures
- enjoy small construction materials
- enjoy dressing up

As the children's hand muscles strengthen they are able to use pencils, pens, paint, paste, brushes and scissors. They need an area outside where these activities can be provided. Easels and tabletop activities are best provided on a verandah or in a shaded area under trees or a pergola. Quite often these activities need to be available outside for children to create objects for their dramatic play, a mobile phone to ring the fire brigade, a letter for the post box, or a menu for their restaurant.

The verandah is also an area where a mat can be rolled out and small construction materials, blocks and train sets can be provided for a group of children to use. Often these activities can be set up on a play platform or in a small amphitheatre.

A woodworking area provides the children with the opportunity to create objects for their play; it also helps develop their hand-eye coordination. Learning to hit the head of a nail instead of their fingers requires practice. A woodworking area is best away from the building as the sound of the hammering can reverberate throughout the whole building. A paved area in front of a storage shed away from the building with a canopy over the door would provide a suitable area.

A large sandpit that will provide enough space for a large group of children is essential. Sandpits with either damp sand or water available are the most used play feature in the outdoors (see Appendix 2). More children use sandpits for longer than any other activity. Damp sand allows children to dig and construct roads and build sand castles with their hands, strengthening their hand muscles.

Social and emotional development

A range of different dress-ups with a variety of fasteners need to be made available for the children. A stand with a range of clothes suitable for both boys and girls conveys to the children that it is appropriate for all children to dress-up if they wish. Many of them will choose clothes suitable to the role they have taken in their dramatic play.

Children in this age group are becoming much more sociable, as is evident in Table 6.3.

TABLE 6.3 SOCIAL AND EMOTIONAL DEVELOPMENT

Children at 42–48 months

- are beginning to interact with others

- play near and talk to other children
- are beginning to take turns and share but need adult help
- are beginning to express feelings such as fear, affection, and humour
- are beginning to show an understanding of being sad or happy
- engage in simple pretend play with or alongside other children
- enjoy dressing-up and dressing dolls
- can follow rules with adult help
- can take part in a short group activity

Children at 48–60 months

- interact with other children
- engage in socio-dramatic play
- engage in cooperative play
- offer things to other children to please them
- enjoy having friends
- can take turns
- participate in group activities both planned and spontaneous
- will assist with packing up

Some children can be overwhelmed by a large group of children and feel more comfortable playing alongside or with one other child. It is useful to have some activities that are suitable for only two or three children so that the more timid children can gradually become part of the group. Finger painting is a very soothing activity and it is useful to have a limit of only two or three children involved in the activity at the same time.

A low table on the lawn under the shade of a tree makes an ideal place for finger painting. Paint can be placed directly on the tabletop and children can use the smooth surface of the table as their canvas. Children need to be given long periods of time to manipulate the paint. The use of several colours at the same time also introduces the children to colour mixing and staff often hear a child call out, 'Hey!, I've made green!!'.

The taking of paper prints from the finger painting tends to end the activity. If a child is upset and in need of a calming experience it would be appropriate not to take a print and allow the child to stay at the activity for longer.

The introduction of guinea pigs or rabbits to nurse or feed is a suitable activity for timid children. Pets need to be kept in enclosures that are safe from predators or vandals and often it is more appropriate to have animals visiting rather than keeping them. Animals need to be in enclosures that are big enough for several children to enter and sit down near the animals, and staff need to stay close so that the children learn to respect and care for the animals.

Staff need to be aware of local requirements for the keeping of pets.

Sometimes children come to the centre after having had an argument with a member of their family or with problems at home and they are unhappy, aggressive or very excited. Very vigorous physical activities are an ideal way to release emotional tensions for some children and the use of a digging area with light sandy loam that children can dig will help release any tensions. Soil is heavier than sand and when children dig, the soil offers resistance causing the children to push harder. As children use their whole bodies to dig, it also helps to develop the leg and arm muscles and whole body coordination.

Digging areas need to be positioned away from the front entrance to the centre as they are not an attractive sight if they are well used. There is usually a corner in most playgrounds that is not being utilised. Children do need a reason to explore and an uninteresting digging area does not inspire activity. Sometimes it is useful to bury colourful stones or bleached bones in the area for children to discover 'treasures' or 'dinosaur's bones'.

Children use dramatic play to explore a variety of known situations and work towards solving problems they may have with those situations in real life. As they spend a great deal of time engaging in socio-dramatic play, the outdoor environment needs to have a variety of areas suitable for this activity. One area is not sufficient as children at this age tend to play in small groups. Several groups may be engaged in socio-dramatic play at the same time, all with different themes and if there is nowhere to make a base there can be conflict.

Children spend a great deal of time setting the scene. They will build a structure with outdoor blocks that, when completed, will be the centre of some dramatic play theme; for example, an ambulance or a boat. Construction often precedes dramatic or socio-dramatic play.

When two groups of children work together to build a structure the final outcome sometimes results in conflict:

- Five children were constructing a vehicle out of large outdoor blocks. The children played cooperatively; they placed a steering wheel in the front with two blocks for the driver's seat and a front passenger and three blocks behind for the other passengers. The children appeared very happy with the end result.

Two of the children began to argue over who would be the driver, eventually one of the children decided to be the passenger in the front seat. But when the driver began to drive and call out 'fire! fire!', all the children in the back seats objected as they thought they were travelling on a bus that was taking them to town. The play disintegrated with children pushing and arguing.

A staff member walked over to the vehicle and asked the children what was happening. After listening to both sides of the argument she asked the fire-fighters if they needed some hoses to put out the fire. When

Metal spades are ideal for use in the digging area as they cut through the soil more easily than plastic ones, but their use raises the question of safety. The centre needs to supply rubber boots to protect the children's feet and the rule of 'no boots, no digging' must be enforced. For safety reasons these spades are not to be used in a sandpit as children dig with their hands and short handled spades and the use of these metal spades would be dangerous.

they replied that they did she directed them to the shed where short lengths of garden hoses were kept. The fire-fighters raced away to the shed and the other children went on their bus to town. ●

There are many areas suitable for children's socio-dramatic play. A play platform that is simple and very flexible can become a house, boat, jetty or an ambulance just by the addition of some furniture or props. An area or structure that looks like nothing and can be added to, to create what the children want, is the most suitable.

A bush cubby created under a clump of bushy trees or shrubs makes an ideal place for dramatic play as does a small amphitheatre. A flat stretch of grass or paving can be converted into a dramatic play space by the use of outdoor blocks, either plastic or wooden or other large construction sets. Large boxes will also become the focus of a dramatic play episode. If the centre has a very large outdoor space then several structures could be useful, giving children a choice. Some dramatic play is of a roving kind where the children shift their base depending on how the play progresses whereas others need a set base where they can come back to or have others visit during the course of the play episode.

A large grassy area outside is useful for staff to set up organised group games from time to time, singing and dancing games, ball games and other types of games that require children to share, take turns and generally enjoy the company of other children.

A large sandpit where large or small groups of children can work together spontaneously constructing castles, roads, rivers and tunnels will give them the opportunity to negotiate, problem-solve, share ideas, and space.

Figure 6.1 A mothers' meeting

Cognitive development

The development levels listed in Table 6.4 can all be fostered by outdoor experiences.

TABLE 6.4 COGNITIVE DEVELOPMENT

Children at 42–48 months

- match colours
- draw a picture and give an explanation
- ask questions on how and why
- learn through imitation
- build enclosures with blocks
- follow directions
- enjoy story books
- enjoy puppets
- enjoy cleaning up
- enjoy finger paint
- enjoy sand and water play
- enjoy playing simple musical instruments
- are interested in plants, animals
- enjoy collecting things
- enjoy being involved in the care of animals
- are interested in planting (quick-growing seeds)
- learn by tasting and smelling
- explore with their senses, such as feeling textures
- enjoy being involved in cooking

Children at 48–60 months

- are developing problem-solving skills
- have developed a large number of concepts
- find abstract concepts such as age, time and space confusing
- are interested in counting and measuring
- are interested in books, letters, and print
- pretend to write, acting out the role of a writer in dramatic play
- begin to write known letters and use them for all written messages
- sort and classify objects
- are interested in nature and science
- are interested in living creatures
- are interested in how things work
- learn through observing and listening as well as through exploration
- follow directions
- can describe their feelings
- speech is easily understood
- are easily distracted

The outdoors can provide a wealth of natural objects such as leaves, rocks, flowers, and seed-pods suitable for children to collect, classify, and compare. An exploratory area with a variety of plants with different textured leaves, different seed-pods and flowers that can be collected by the children would be of constant interest; a winding path through such an area could lead to a bush cubby where children could either engage in dramatic play, or use the area for examining their collections.

A sensory garden of plants with a variety of textures, perfumes and coloured flowers could be planted in another area of the playground. A narrow winding path through the garden allows the children to experience the different perfumes as their clothes brush against the plants as they walk.

Children are very interested in birds and the planting of bird-attracting plants will ensure that native birds will enter the playground. The study of native birds in the surrounding trees is of more interest to the children than caged birds whose activities are severely restricted within the confines of a cage. Bird feeders could be made by the children at the woodwork table and suitable food could be placed in the feeders by the children when the interest is there. Be aware though that continued feeding of native birds tends to make the birds reliant on the food, which can cause problems during holiday periods. Occasional feeding of birds is preferred. Nests in trees fascinate children and they can follow the growth of the baby birds through their observations and the use of resource books.

A garden area specifically for the children will provide them with the opportunity to sow seeds, observe and record growth and perhaps, depending on the type of plants, use the vegetables or fruit in cooking projects. A long narrow garden bed is best for young children as they do not have to walk over the garden bed to look after their plants. Small paths in the garden beds approximately every metre mean that the children can reach all of the garden without treading on it. Watering cans readily available to the children will provide the plants with some water, however it is wise not to rely entirely on the children's watering and a simple watering system in the children's garden will ensure the plants have plenty of water. The garden should also be in a sunny position as most vegetables and flowers need sun to thrive.

As children of this age are very interested in print it is useful to supply writing tools, pencils, pens, or crayons and small pads, paper or old forms in a variety of areas in the outdoors. It is useful for the children to act out the role of a writer and label the seeds they plant. A table, chair, telephone and a pad and pencils placed on the verandah or in the shade of a tree will encourage children to use the area whenever they feel they need to write. As their knowledge of print increases their 'writing' will reveal the changes. Most roles children take in their socio-dramatic play episodes require writing. Prop boxes with writing equipment can be placed in a play platform with furniture and other props to extend the play. Placing books and posters relevant to the current interests of the children on the verandah will also enhance their learning. Print is relevant as much in the outdoors as it is indoors.

Socio-dramatic play becomes more complex between the ages of four and five years and the children require access to more props and furniture to support their play. It is useful to have boxes set up with articles suitable for particular play themes that the children can access. A shelf in an equipment shed in the playground could be known to the children as their shelf and they could be encouraged to help themselves to the boxes and be responsible for packing up and returning the boxes to the shelf at the end of the day. Props boxes for hospital play, office play, home play, fire stations and fire engines and other common play themes would enrich the children's play and support their developing independence and responsibilities.

Children's current interests can be extended by setting up a dramatic play area; for example, as a shop with scales, paper, pencils, paper bags, wrapping paper, articles to sell, telephones etc.

In the sandpit, pulleys with buckets on the ends provide weighing experiences and help to develop concepts of heavier, lighter, balance, lower and higher as well as providing props for construction of roads play.

A water play trough could be placed on a level grassed area or a hard surface near a garden so that the water can be emptied onto the garden when no longer in use. Alternatively a large container of water could be placed in the sandpit where children could experiment with floating and sinking and the concepts of full and empty.

Ensure that all containers of water are emptied before staff leave the area.

Suggestions for staff

Table 6.6 provides staff with some ideas to facilitate children's development.

TABLE 6.6 SUGGESTIONS FOR STAFF WORKING WITH CHILDREN 42–60 MONTHS

- Be aware of the interests of the children as well as their developmental needs. It is through their interests that staff can encourage children to engage in many of the activities that they may not normally be interested in. Plan activities that incorporate the interests of groups of children or individuals. Some children will never dig in a digging area, but if there might be dinosaur bones in the soil and they are interested in dinosaurs, they will dig or if there might be hidden treasures, they will dig.
- Make time to play ball with the children, they need staff help and interest to succeed.
- Be prepared to add loose materials to the fixed pieces of play equipment in the playground. If the equipment is such that nothing can be added make sure that obstacle courses are set up with boards, ladders, slide boards, balance beams, and collapsible tunnels. Change them regularly to retain children's interest so that they want to explore the new set-up.
- Help the children with their swinging. Some children can pump up a swing quite well but, for those who are having trouble, be prepared to stand by the swing a tell them to move their feet 'backwards', ' forwards' at the appropriate

time until they get the rhythm. Be prepared to help them until it becomes natural to them.

- Set up art materials on tables outside in the shade for those children who wish to engage in creative activities.
- Clay is a wonderful medium. However, the clay must always be soft, so store it in a container with a lid with a damp cloth around it. If it dries out it can be reconstituted but children cannot work with hard clay. The clay table needs an adult either in the area or close by for children to want to spend time at the activity. It is a good time to talk about the texture of the clay or any other topic of interest to the child or children. Plastic scrapers, plastic knives, sticks and gumnuts add to the appeal of the area. Sit at the table if another staff member is available to help with the other children.
- An adult needs to be close by when woodwork is first introduced to ensure that children know the safety rules. Sometimes children need staff to start hammering the nail and for them to finish it. Always use soft wood. Bottle tops, strips of leather, fur and corks are interesting additions to this area.
- Make sure the sand in the sandpit is damp enough for children to construct or that they have access to enough water to make the sand damp.
- Often staff see finger painting as an art activity rather than one that releases tensions and gives children the opportunity to interact with one or two children and the opportunity to colour mix if two different colours are presented.

Be aware of children who have difficulty playing with others but want to join in and are not accepted. If a child acts out the role of a scary creature it is often in an attempt to frighten the other children into letting them play. These children need help. Choose a role for the child and help the child enter the play. Stay nearby for support.

- If a print is made of the finger-painting it usually ends the activity, which sometimes is a shame as the children are just beginning to talk to the other children when they have to stop. In many situations, particularly when the children are not creating but enjoying the tactile experience, taking a print is not necessary. Cleaning up the finger paint on the table should be part of the activity and each child needs to be aware that they have a responsibility to clean up after they have finished.
- When presenting dress-ups from other cultures make sure you involve the family and or the children from that family in any discussions on the clothes. This will help their self-esteem and a feeling of acceptance.
- When establishing a digging area dig in sandy loam, place some large- to medium-sized moss rocks or a fallen tree trunk in the middle that children can dig under, around and in between to add to the interest.
- When choosing plants for the children's garden try and plant something that the centre's pet can eat so that the children can be actively involved in the growing, picking and feeding processes.
- The role of the adult in children's dramatic play is very important. You need to be aware of the play skills of the players and act accordingly. Your first role is to set up the environment so that it can happen. Once the scene is set by the children follow the play from behind, providing props, information or reference books when appropriate. Respect the children's play, they must own it, not the adult.

Planning the outdoor play environment

As the children's social skills develop they are very keen to play with other children. It is important to them to have friends and to be able to play with them. Activities and play features in the playground must provide for small groups of children to play together as well as catering for the more timid and quiet children who wish to be alone for a while or with one other special friend. Areas for quiet and boisterous play must be provided to cater for all the children's needs.

A playground full of the more natural elements such as sand, soil, water, plants, animals, insects and birds will offer the children the opportunity to explore and discover. Nature is ever-changing, therefore there is always something new for curious children to discover.

To illustrate a concept design for this group we'll use the concept design in Figure 6.2. This preschool was established many years ago and has many well-established trees. However, the playground was uninteresting and needed to be redeveloped. The following concept is the result of staff, parents, children and a consultant working together to provide an interesting, challenging and absorbing outdoor learning environment.

A cement path leads from the front gate to the building. On the northern side of the path is a two-sectioned sandpit. The original square one proved to be too small so the second section was built with large moss rocks around the edge. Some of the rocks are flat and suitable for adults or children to use as seats when interacting with children in the sandpit. The western side of the old sandpit section is edged with a rockery garden planted with different perfumed plants. The children use the flowers and leaves to decorate their castles or to add to their 'cooking' in the sandpit. The entrance to the new section of the sandpit is clearly visible from the door of the building.

A water feature on the northern side of the sandpit empties water into the new sandpit section on a wide front. The water flows under an existing clatterbridge, around a large rock and into the sandpit in two places so that more than one group of children have access to the water at the same time. The water supply is from a vandal-proof tap, which can be turned on when required. The vandal-proof tap reduces the possibility of water being used without adult supervision, at the weekends and holidays.

On the eastern side of the old square sandpit is a mound with steps leading from the sandpit to the top of the mound. The mound has a slide at the top, which faces south, away from facing the sun, and a grassy side for children to roll down on the eastern side. The surrounding fences are lined with bird-attracting trees. Their songs can be heard as the children play in the sandpit nearby.

West of the sandpit is a low wooden play platform with three sections. Shade cloth can be attached to the high poles in six of the corners when required (see Figure 6.2) Movable boards and ladders can be added to the galvanised bars attached to one of the front sections (see an example in Figure 1.6). The back of the platform has safety guard rail fencing to create a cosy area for

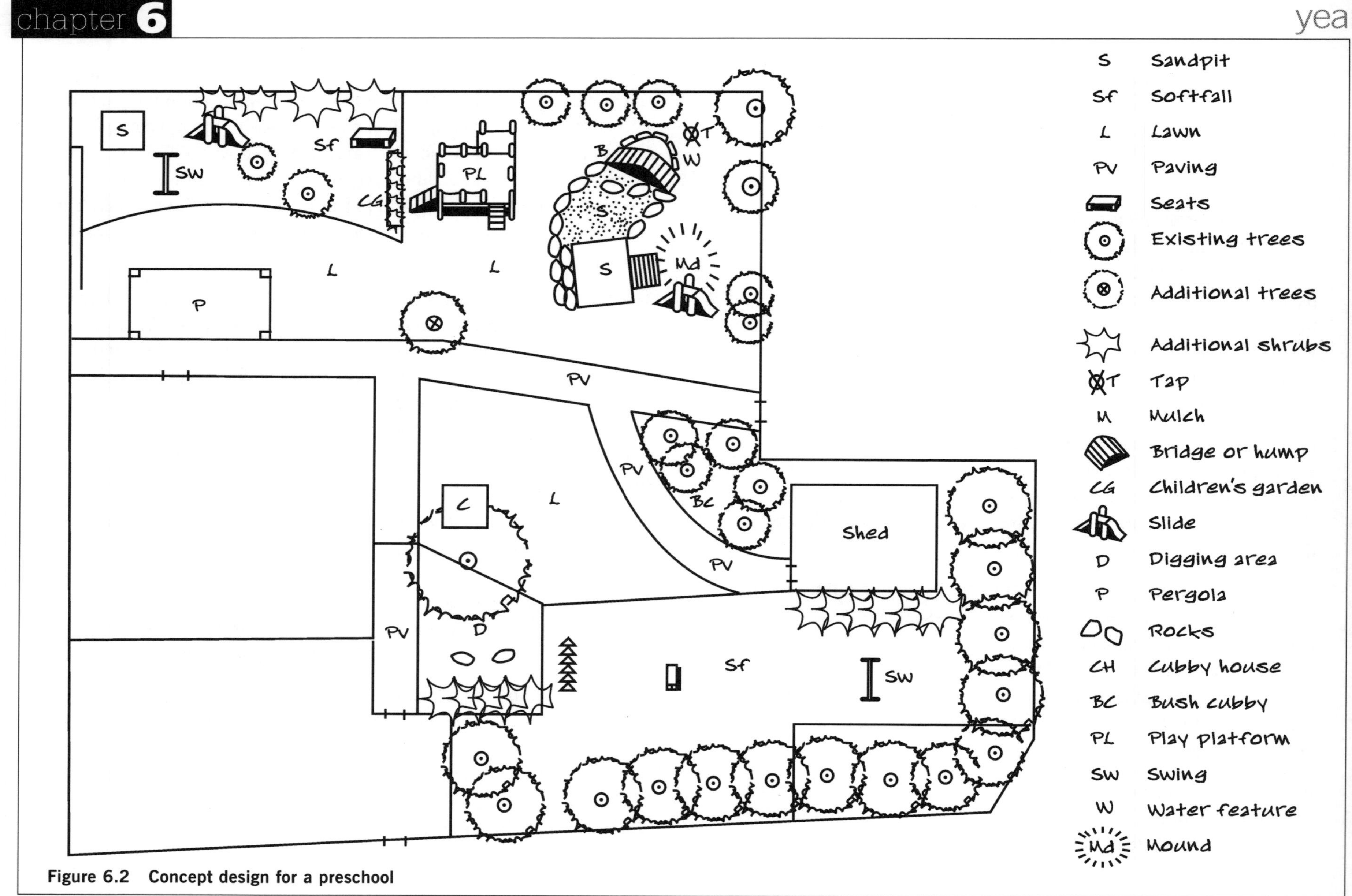

Figure 6.2 Concept design for a preschool

children to engage in dramatic or construction play depending on the current needs and interests of the children.

On the southern side of the entrance gate from the car park is a cubby of bushy shrubs. Garden mulch has been placed on the ground to stop any dust or mud. This bush cubby provides a quiet place for dramatic play, a place for 'bird watchers' to hide or a place for picnics with a rug on the ground and plastic picnic plates and cups. Soft-fall material from the nearby climbing area makes good 'food'.

A curved path leads off the entrance path to the equipment shed, which stores prop boxes, movable boards and ladders, sand equipment and other loose materials that will enhance children's play. Hardy perfumed plants such as rosemary, lavender and some herbs have been planted on the western side of the path to create a sense of adventure as children walk through to the bush cubby on the eastern side.

On the western side of the curved path is a small cubbyhouse low to the ground surrounded by lawn. This house was originally in the soft-fall area, on stilts with a slide attached to the front section. It did not conform to safety standards, the house section was seldom used, staff could not reach children when they were up in the cubby section and staff and parents felt it was unsafe. The slide was removed and placed in the mound and the house was lowered to ground level and placed on the lawn so that children could use it. It only appeals to the children when furniture is placed inside. Props like paper, pencils and a telephone have proved to be very popular with the children when the house becomes an office, a hospital and a shop. After observing a new house being built in the street, the children decided it needed plumbing pipes and wiring just like the new house. With staff support this was achieved to the children's satisfaction.

Because the cubby is so small staff often place mats on the lawn with outdoor wooden blocks available for children to build extensions to their house or hospital.

South of the cubbyhouse is the digging area. Light sandy loam has been dug into the existing soil to ensure it is light enough for children to dig. Two large moss rocks have been placed in the area so that children can dig in between, around, behind and in front of the rocks. Plumbing pipes are often used in the area with children laying pipes between the rocks. Sometimes the pipes are extended to the nearby cubby as plumbing to the house. Water in the digging area adds to the appeal. A vandal-proof tap was installed to allow staff to regulate the supply of water in the area.

East of the digging area is the soft-fall area where a variety of fixed climbing apparatus has been placed. At the extreme end of this area a double swing frame provides for different types of swings to be attached depending on the skills of the children wanting to use the swings (see Chapter 1).

The building is surrounded on two sides with a verandah. A woodwork table stocked with hammers, nails and other woodworking tools is available. Children often make objects at this table to support their play, for example, boats for the water in the sand, mobile phones for their ambulance and animals for their farm. The verandah also provides places for mats with construction toys when appropriate. A paved area immediately out from the entrance door of the centre shaded by a pergola provides another area for tabletop activities.

This particular preschool has playgroup sessions operating at the same time as the preschool. These are run by the parents and cater for children under five. A building in the north-west corner opens into a separate playground that has been set up for these children, although the children are welcome to use the preschool playground and equipment. A small sandpit, swings and a slide are available for the children with parent supervision. Bench seats in the area ensure that parents have a place to sit while they watch their children at play and socialise with other parents.

A narrow children's garden at the end of the playgroup section acts as a barrier to small children running into the more boisterous play of the older children. This garden is planted and cared for by the preschool children with support from the staff.

chapter 7

Outdoor areas for children aged five to eight years

The outdoor areas in schools need to include a wide range of activities to cater for the needs and interests of children during their recess and lunchtime breaks as well as for use as extensions to the school curriculum. Children need the opportunity to be quiet or active, to socialise or to be alone and to be involved in sporting activities appropriate to the age and current interests of both genders.

In most schools the use of outdoor play areas differs considerably from those in preschools and child-care centres. Instead of the playground being seen as part of the educational program it is used mainly for recreational use with the main focus being on sport and play equipment designed to cater for the children's physical development.

Very little attention is given to the children's social and emotional needs or in fact their cognitive development. It is important for staff and school councils to recognise the potential learning opportunities the outdoors offer. The National Statements and Profiles include many activities that are more suited to the outdoors than a classroom.

The social and emotional wellbeing of school-age children influences their self-esteem and can affect their performance in the classroom and in life generally. Children who feel a failure in the playground often carry that impression with them wherever they are and it intrudes into all facets of their life. It is through positive social interactions that social skills develop and self-esteem increases.

Children (five to six years)

Children at the age of five and six are in a transition stage of learning from 'hands on' experiences to more complex and abstract learning, which is often facilitated by teachers, and for this reason many of the activities found in preschools are still suitable for this age group.

Gross motor development

Table 7.1 lists developmental areas that can be fostered by organised sport and physical education sessions as well as during recess and lunchtime breaks.

TABLE 7.1 GROSS MOTOR DEVELOPMENT
Children at 5–6 years can:
• run in a coordinated way, light on their feet
• gallop
• skip using alternate feet
• walk on a balance beam
• climb well
• jump forward five or six times without stumbling
• jump over objects
• hop several metres on each foot
• kick a large ball through the air, kick a drop kick and run up to and kick a moving ball
• hang from bar using overhead grip for a few seconds
• throw a tennis ball
• throw a large ball against a wall and catch it
• catch with their hands a large ball that is thrown by others from several metres
• hit a large ball with a bat or stick when the ball is bounced

A grassy area or an oval suitable for sporting activities provides a place for children to run, gallop, hop and jump as well as practise their kicking. The problem often is that the older children who are more proficient in their kicking and running tend to take over the area leaving very little space for the younger children. However, as the younger children do not kick balls very far a smaller grassed area could be used.

A hard surface of either paving, cement or asphalt is necessary for children to play some ball games. If space is limited, a brick wall without windows or doors or a specially constructed self-standing board provides children with the opportunity to throw or hit balls up against a wall by themselves or with one other child. Skipping with or without a rope also needs a hard surface.

Both boys and girls in this age group love to climb. Climbing structures need to include opportunities for children to climb up, over and under bars, slide, hang by their hands and legs, and use balance beams and clatterbridges that provide balancing experiences. Any climbing structure must have impact-absorbent materials underneath and out to the sides no less than the maximum potential fall height to conform to the Australian Standards. Children in this age group often over-estimate their abilities on climbing equipment and take incredible risks therefore it is imperative that the depth of soft-fall is appropriate to the height of the equipment and the size of the child.

Children learn to control the movement of their bodies, the ability to stop, start and change direction while engaging in games of chasings where they experience the excitement of the chase and flight. An area with bushy shrubs that children can hide in and dodge around and behind will contribute to a more interesting and challenging game.

Fine motor development

Table 7.2 lists areas that can be developed through a variety of art and craft activities.

TABLE 7.2 FINE MOTOR DEVELOPMENT

Children at 5–6 years:
• use scissors
• have an adult grasp of pencils
• can use brushes with paint or paste appropriately
• are beginning to write, copy shapes
• can do up buttons and zips
• are beginning to tie laces with help

An outdoor area paved and shaded by trees or a pergola provides a very flexible area suitable for a wide range of art and craft activities. It needs to be placed in a quiet area so that children are not distracted by activities nearby and creations can be left in the area to dry without being damaged. Easels or tables and chairs could be placed in the area depending on the need. If children are going to spend a whole lesson time in this area the shade needs to be one that blocks out ultraviolet rays. (See Chapter 1 for a discussion on shade.)

A children's garden needs to be established with the children where they can label the plants and record the growth. The garden needs to be in the sun for most plants to grow and have a tap nearby so that the children can be responsible for watering the plants.

A sandpit with damp sand provides children with the opportunity to dig, fill containers and construct with or without tools. A water feature entering the sandpit ensures the sand is damp and suitable for manipulating. Dry sand blows in windy weather and is unsuitable for manipulation and construction. The younger children with weaker hand muscles who are having difficulty cutting with scissors and using pencils and brushes will benefit from digging in damp sand with their hands, as damp sand offers resistance, which exercises the muscles. The sandpit needs to be well shaded. The planting of low shrubs around two or three sides of the sandpit will provide a cosy area conducive to sustained, quality play.

Social and emotional development

The development of the skills listed in Table 7.3 is extremely important to children of this age as they need to feel accepted by their peers.

TABLE 7.3 SOCIAL AND EMOTIONAL DEVELOPMENT
Children at 5–6 years:
• need to have a friend or friends, choose own friends, form small groups
• enjoy being read to
• enjoy dramatic play with others
• are interested in creating fantasy worlds in their dramatic play
• enjoy re-enacting stories from television, film or books
• enjoy jokes
• engage with others in cooperative play involving group decisions and role assignments
• enjoy acting out roles in dramatic play
• enjoy sand and water play
• have interests that are more gender selective

Children in the early years of school come with a wide range of experiences that determine their skills and interests. Many have had very little experience interacting with children of their own age and find it very difficult to make friends. Some are skilled in dramatic play, some have invented imaginary friends or imaginary situations; often the television provides them with their ideas. Some children are overwhelmed by the large school playground, the number of children and the lack of adult support. It is important that these children have cosy areas where they feel secure and quiet places where they can learn to interact with one or two others with similar interests.

Paths that lead to a bush cubby, long grass where children can pretend to be 'Hercules looking for baby monsters', or a garden area where they can look for fairies, provide children with the opportunity to explore and make discoveries. A variety of areas suitable for use by children engaged in socio-dramatic play can be developed around the edge of an oval. For example, a path with a small bridge and a dry creek bed provides an area for a wide range of play themes. A boat, with decking in the shape of a jetty next to it, surrounded by sand allows children to 'swim' in the sand, climb on board the boat and sail off after pirates.

A small amphitheatre or any other semi-enclosed area also provides children with the opportunity for dramatic play. Prop-boxes on a variety of themes should be made available with a monitoring system where the children are responsible for recording the borrowing and return of the equipment. An amphitheatre also provides a place for story reading.

Seating needs to be provided in a variety of forms throughout the play areas — bench seats for spectators, where children can watch sporting activities or watch other children at play, a semi circle of tree trunk seats, a 'U' shaped formation of seats or a small amphitheatre where children have eye contact with one another facilitate interactions with others.

Cognitive development

Development in many of the areas listed in Table 7.4 can be fostered by both indoor and outdoor experiences.

TABLE 7.4 COGNITIVE DEVELOPMENT

Children at 5–6 years:

- can indicate spatial positions — over, under, between, through, around corner
- indicate top and bottom
- indicate left and right
- can print own name
- show interest in writing and reading words
- use scissors and paint purposefully
- have noticeably increased attention span
- learn through instruction
- can ignore distractions when interested
- are interested in how things work
- are interested in time
- are interested in product as well as process in art
- engage in dramatic play, construction play and make models that are more realistic
- are interested in nature, science

A children's garden provides staff with the opportunity to plan maths and science experiences in the outdoors. Children can measure the height of plants and the weight of produce from a vegetable garden. They can observe and study life cycles and the role of a variety of garden creatures such as caterpillars, snails, ants and bees in the food chain.

A study of birds can be enhanced by the planting of bird-attracting trees and shrubs and the placing of bird feeders and water in the area. Children can discover through observation which birds are honey eaters, seed eaters, or meat eaters, and whether they walk, run or hop. All the information can be recorded by the children.

The planting of trees and shrubs with different textured leaves and bark and flowers of different shapes, colours and perfume can all be classified and sorted. Plant them along the edges of paths and around the oval or grassed areas. Science, art and craft activities can be planned around these plants.

Use a pergola beam over a sandpit to attach pulleys on a rope with buckets at each end. This will provide children with the experience of weighing, confirming concepts of heavier and lighter and balance. Large containers filled with water either in a sandpit or in a water trough will provide activities such as measuring, floating and sinking. If a water trough is to be used, leftover water should be emptied onto a garden area to ensure no water is wasted.

An area for composting of weeds from the garden and food scraps from recess and lunchtime will introduce the children to environmental issues.

Children (six to eight years)

Gross motor development

Children in this age group are beginning to be more involved in sporting activities and participate in the types of activities shown in Table 7.5.

TABLE 7.5 GROSS MOTOR DEVELOPMENT

Children between the ages of 6–8 years can:

- climb up and down climbing equipment independently
- throw a tennis ball overarm in direction of a target
- strike with a bat a ball thrown from 1.5 m
- throw and catch accurately
- bounce a large ball with one hand
- run easily, picking up objects from the ground while running
- coordinate movements in time with music
- jump over a rope 15 cm high with feet together
- jump forward feet together
- skip with or without a rope
- walk considerable distances
- run some distance without tiring including races with a start and finish
- play sporting games with rules
- find long periods of sitting more tiring than running activities

A large number of children in this age range are beginning to engage in sporting activities. An oval or a large grassed area will provide space for the large number of children wanting to join in running races, jumping hurdles, kicking footballs, throwing balls and playing cricket. Movable goal posts and soccer nets give children the opportunity to practise kicking goals. The posts and nets can be removed when not required. Balls, bats and stumps should be readily available so that everyone who wants to play has the opportunity.

A hard surface away from the main buildings and paths will allow children to skip with ropes without being interrupted by the through traffic. Handball courts, netball and basketball hoops are needed to provide activities for those who are interested in ball games but prefer to play in small groups.

Children of this age like to dance to music and practise dance routines. Access to a tape recorder and a CD player will enable children or staff to play recorded music for this purpose.

Climbing equipment for this age group needs to be made up of gymnastic type components, such as horizontal ladders and Roman rings or triangles and clatterbridges. These will strengthen the leg muscles, develop the upper body and increase balancing skills. By the time children turn eight years old they become disinterested in equipment, and are more interested in sport and socialising.

A sanded area alongside an oval provides children with the opportunity to practise long-jumps.

In 1985 a national survey was conducted to gain information about the health and fitness of Australian children. The findings (published by the Curriculum Development Centre, Canberra) were that students were not as fit as they could be and that there was lower participation in physical activities by girls compared with boys.

The Australian Council for Health, Physical Education and Recreation (ACHPER) was concerned that students were not receiving enough regular, vigorous physical activity. A National Fitness Award Scheme was set up to encourage all Australian children to reach a minimum level of fitness by 1990.

In 1997 a study was carried out by the School of Physical Education, Exercise and Sport Studies at the University of South Australia using the same format as the 1985 study. The findings in this study were that children were taller, heavier and fatter and less fit than those in the 1985 study.

Of particular concern in both studies was the findings that girls engage in less vigorous physical activities than boys. The boys used sports equipment more often than the girls and tended to dominate the oval and the climbing equipment. Although most of the students in the survey were over eight years old this trend is still present in schools and is evident at earlier ages. It is important therefore that schools monitor the use of the playground facilities and ensure there is an equal opportunity for both sexes to engage in a variety of vigorous physical activities.

Social and emotional development

Friendship groups influence children's school experiences both in the playground and the classroom (see Table 7.6).

TABLE 7.6 SOCIAL AND EMOTIONAL DEVELOPMENT

Children between the ages of 6–8 years:
• enjoy special friends
• prefer friends of the same gender
• are very interested in their peer group
• enjoy group activities
• are able to play cooperatively
• do not happily accept losing a game
• are concerned about what they consider is 'fair'
• enjoy being read to
• enjoy socio-dramatic play, re-enacting shows they have seen
• enjoy acting out plays they have written themselves

As friendships are of prime importance, facilities must foster interactions between children. Seats need to be placed all around the play area so that small groups can sit and interact. Place seats in semi-circles or 'U' shapes so that children sit facing one another. If the seating is all around a tree, children do not get eye contact with their friends as easily. Bench seats are ideal for use by spectators around an oval or a tennis or basketball court, but are not appropriate for socialisation.

Areas of firm dirt in a secluded area around an oval allow for games of marbles and sanded areas are useful for toy cars and the construction of fantasy-type scenes, all activities where small groups and special friends can play and work together. Bushy shrubs and medium-sized trees with a path winding through will provide an exploratory track where children can go adventuring.

Children who want to re-enact plays or films they have seen or even invent their own plays would enjoy a shaded paved area, an amphitheatre or a stage constructed of decking with several long, wide steps up the front for grand exits and entrances. If a space is left clear in front of this structure it can be used for more serious school performances where the audience can sit out the front on chairs or on the grass.

Quiet shady grassed areas provide a place where children can sit together and share their dolls, puppets and toy cars, or do magic tricks. Paths with perfumed plants either side leading to a quiet sitting area will appeal to the children's senses. Choose hardy plants with different textures leaves and lots of flowers so that the children feel free to pick the flowers. Daisy type flowers are ideal for making daisy chains.

Cognitive development

Table 7.7 highlights the shift in children's abilities.

TABLE 7.7 COGNITIVE DEVELOPMENT

Children between the ages of 6–8 years:
• experience a significant shift in cognitive abilities
• begin to understand conservation of liquid quantity, number, length
• can maintain a focus for an extended period of time
• have the ability to think about and solve a wide range of problems
• are beginning to understand other people's points of view
• enjoy mathematical activities
• can carry out a range of conservational tasks
• have concepts of number and one-to-one correspondence well developed
• have skills in classification, seriation is developing
• enjoy reading and writing
• are interested in nature and science
• have increasing interest in the world around them

There are many experiences that can be provided in the outdoors that support the curriculum areas included in the National Statements and Profiles. Some of the ideas raised below can be in the play areas of the school or in a quiet withdrawal area where staff can take groups of children outside at lesson time.

Sanded areas in the form of a sandpit or shallow sand used for long-jump practice provide children with the opportunity to weigh wet and dry sand, compare soil and sand in terms of weight, and textures, and learn about the use of both mediums in construction. They can discuss and record the differences.

A quiet sitting area with a fish or frog pond either in the centre or close by gives children the opportunity to study creatures and plants that live in water as well as having a calming effect on all who watch the movement of fish in water. Place a sundial in a sunny area, surround it with perfumed plants with a path up to the sundial so that children can see how early civilisations used the sun to tell the time.

A children's garden provides the children with the opportunity to plant vegetables, herbs, flowering and fruiting plants and record the date planted, measure the plant growth, and chart the results. It also provides opportunities to harvest and taste the produce either raw or in a cooking activity. Vegetables, herbs and fruit from other cultures need to be included to increase the children's awareness of other cultures and the types of food common to that culture. Seeds can be collected and planted in different conditions and differences in growth recorded. The leaves and flowers from different plants can be compared and discussed in terms of size, shape, colour and texture. The bees, butterflies and birds attracted to the garden can be recorded and their function discussed. A bird bath and bird feeders will encourage birds into the garden.

Involve the children in the planting of trees and shrubs indigenous to the area and establish a food trail with bush tucker plants as part of an environmental program.

It will depend on the land available, however a small scale planting would be sufficient to provide the children with valuable experience in land care and a better understanding of the foods eaten by Indigenous Australians and the early settlers.

An area should be set aside for composting. All the food scraps from around the school can be collected and emptied into a compost bin to reduce the amount of landfill and provide compost for the vegetable garden at a later date. The use of a bin rather than a pit reduces the possibility of attracting vermin into the area. The setting up of a worm farm to be used in the decomposition process will be of great interest and a learning experience for all the children.

Encourage children to write their own plays and use a quiet area, preferable slightly elevated, such as a mounded area, an amphitheatre or timber decking stage, to present their works to their peers.

Suggestions for staff

Table 7.8 lists some ideas for staff to consider that are suitable as outdoor experiences.

TABLE 7.8 SUGGESTIONS FOR STAFF WORKING WITH CHILDREN 5–8 YEARS

Gardens

- allow space for a class planting area
- discuss the needs of plants
- plant vegetables, herbs and flowers, observe and predict growth, make a chart of the growth
- discuss features of plants such as deciduous, evergreen, poisonous or edible
- collect and dry samples of flowers and seeds from the garden and create a book about the garden, either individually or as a class project.
- introduce parts of a plant, for example the roots and their function
- cut or pick produce from the garden, explore the textures, smells and tastes
- use produce in cooking
- introduce cooking from other cultures and identify some of the plants used in favourite recipes from other cultures (have family members come and cook a traditional dish)
- use petals and leaves for counting and measuring activities
- use the garden as a setting for the re-enactment of a well known story or one written by the children
- read stories about adventures in gardens, such as *Alice's Adventures in Wonderland* by Lewis Carroll, *The Secret Garden* by Frances Hodgson Burnett.
- have a tea party in the garden

Trees and shrubs

- look at different types of trees and shrubs and their uses, such as shelter from sun, wind and rain

- plant or create a bush cubby
- look at cultures that use natural resources for housing
- make models of different bush houses
- make a list of creatures that make their homes in trees or shrubs
- explore the different eating habits of those creatures
- discuss camouflage, identify creatures that use camouflage to protect themselves

Rocks

- collect different types of rocks from the playground
- look at the textures, colour when wet and dry and record the differences
- introduce the term erosion and what causes erosion
- discuss the effect on different rocks
- discuss the gradual decomposition from rock to soil
- discuss volcanoes dormant and active and their effect
- discuss rock formations of caves
- look at cultures ancient and modern that use stone carvings and rock paintings, have children paint their own rocks
- study the use of rocks in today's culture

Sand and soil areas

- investigate and discuss earthworms, different species, such as the bloodworm, and composting
- constructions with sand promote problem-solving skills and collaboration between children
- collect sand and soil from different locations and compare
- investigate the layers of soil that make up the earth's crust
- study the different animals and plant life that existed on the different layers throughout the ages
- discuss the formation of fossils
- study the storytelling of other cultures such as sand pictures and the Aboriginal oral tradition
- discuss paints made from soils of different regions, use Aboriginal art as one example
- have children paint with different soils

Water

- test and discuss objects that float and sink
- carry out simple experiments to demonstrate evaporation, record rate of evaporation in different situations
- identify animals and insects that live in or near lakes, rivers, streams and waterfalls
- identify those that live in salt water and those in fresh

- look at the use of water for irrigation
- look at ancient cultures' reliance on water for transportation
- discuss issues of conservation
- explore issues of pollution
- discuss the establishment of wetlands and the role of wetlands
- visit a recently developed wetland

Planning the outdoor play environment

The concept design shown in Figure 7.1 is stage one of a school playground redevelopment and only includes a small section of the total playground. It was the result of input from children at the planning stage. Children's ideas were collected through conversations with them at recess and lunchtime, their drawings of the play features they would like included and from observations of their playground behaviour. (See Chapter 3 for staff's and students' wish lists for their playground.)

This school is fortunate to have a separate area for the junior primary-aged children that includes a small oval, a mounded area in front of the classrooms and space for climbing, handball courts and basketball rings either side of the mounded area. There are future plans to include some of the features that would support curriculum activities behind the classrooms.

The section to be discussed is an area approximately 50 m long around the north-eastern side of the oval.

A sandpit with a water feature is positioned in the north-eastern corner so that children using the sand can see a large part of the playing area including the children using the oval. The sandpit at ground level is a quiet place for younger children to play until they feel comfortable moving into the more vigorous play on the oval. Water gently flows over and around smooth rocks to enter the sandpit providing children with damp sand for construction work and the opportunity for small groups to work together to channel the water, build bridges, or a dam. The water supply is by a vandal-proof tap, which allows staff to regulate the water by removing the top. It also makes it harder for vandals during weekends and holidays to use the water if the tap top has been removed.

In front of the sandpit is a path of non-slip pavers where sand can be swept back into the sandpit. Over the sandpit is a generous set of sails that shade the whole area protecting the children from the UV rays.

A path of compacted building sand leads from the sandpit along the eastern side of the oval, winding in and out of well-established trees. A set of three bench seats have been placed under the shade of two large trees. The seats are positioned so that children can

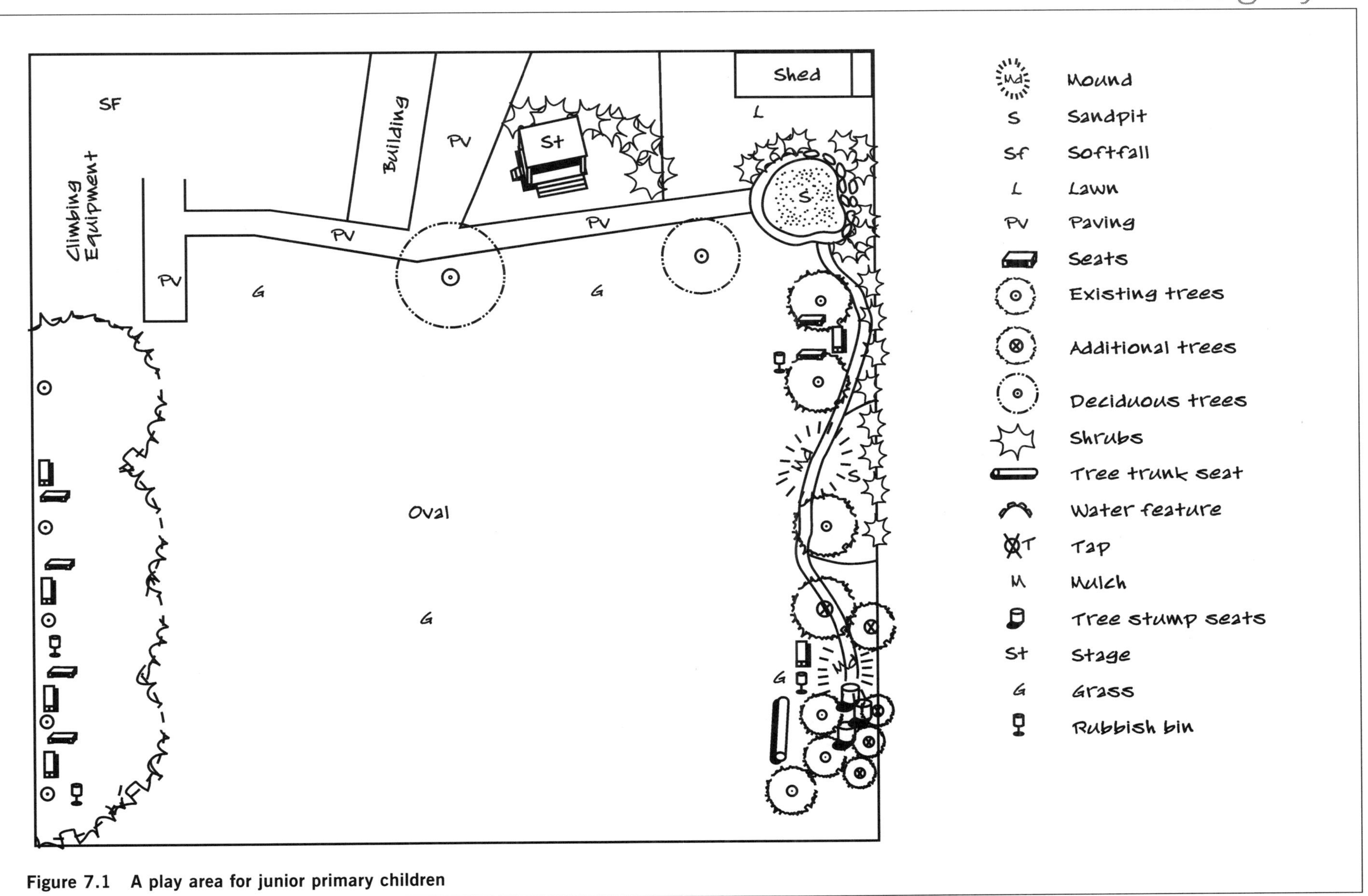

Figure 7.1 A play area for junior primary children

watch the activities on the oval but still maintain eye contact with friends sitting on an opposite bench seat. A rubbish bin has been placed nearby so that children can put their rubbish in the bin instead of having to walk back to near the classroom to put rubbish in a bin. This resulted from complaints by the children during a rubbish clean-up around the oval.

The path continues to wind around, this time up a low mound and down the other side giving the children the opportunity to have fun in a game of chasings while at the same time exercising leg muscles as they run along the track. The top of the mound can be used as a lookout in dramatic play as well as acting as a barrier between a shallow sanded area and the grassy oval. The sanded area is large enough for children to use in their dramatic play with cars and small dolls or to practise long-jumps.

Another mound closer to the fence is positioned just north of a bush cubby that has some tree stump seats in garden mulch to provide a secret place for children to play. The bush cubby is placed at the end of the area designated for the junior primary-aged children. Extra shrub plantings ensure that the area has a cosy feel but children can still be seen from the oval side.

In front of the last mound another bench seat allows for more spectator activity and a large tree trunk on the oval side of the bush cubby provides another area for children to meet. There is also another rubbish bin. Before redevelopment many of the children would gather in groups around the soccer nets, each group claiming a part of the nets as their base, often resulting in conflict over territory.

All along the fence line bushy shrubs are planted to soften the look of the iron fence and to give the whole area a more cosy inviting appearance.

At the northern end of the oval a low decking stage is constructed to provide a place for children to play at recess and lunchtime or to act out plays or familiar stories as part of their classroom activities. This stage also has generous sails placed over the top to provide shelter from the hot sun especially in the middle of the day at lunch time when all the children are outside.

conclusion

Where to now?

Once a playground has been established and the landscaping, play features and fixed equipment are in place, thought must be given to the maintenance of this outdoor environment. Management needs to set up a program that will ensure the playground is maintained in a safe and attractive condition.

Information on the maintenance and safety of playgrounds can be found in the Australian Standards, or in the book published by NSW Health Department, *Playground Safety* (see Chapter 1 and the Bibliography for details).

It does not matter how attractive a playground is, it will not hold the interest of young children for long unless there are a variety of props or adjuncts available. Nicholson (1971) described materials, such as props and adjuncts, that could be manipulated and used in a variety of ways as 'loose parts', and it is the use of these loose parts that adds to the interest. For example, a sandpit is not very interesting until it has buckets, spades, trucks, cars and water; and play platforms or cubbyhouses are just empty spaces without furniture and/or dress-ups. The use of these loose parts extends the possible play opportunities and allows the child to be creative, and engage in sustained quality play.

It was disappointing for me to hear a staff member at a centre with a redeveloped playground claim: 'now that the playground has been redeveloped to include natural play features as well as appropriate manufactured equipment, there is no need to add anything to it, and packing up is a breeze'.

Children do need to be able to manipulate and change things in their environment and the addition of loose parts gives them that opportunity. Jones (1989, p. 15) describes a situation in an early childhood playground where there were no loose parts. The children spent most of the outdoor time running around, wrestling in the sandpit and asking when it was lunchtime. When plastic animals and boxes were introduced, the play changed and the children settled down and engaged in a variety of activities involving the animals. A zoo was built, enclosures were made for the animals, some animals were washed and fed, others were taken for a ride and some were hidden under leaves.

The loose parts that are added need not be expensive toys, they can be natural or manufactured things such as pebbles, small stones, planks of wood, rope, baskets, picnic gear, wood chips, twigs and dress-ups — the possibilities are endless. No playground should be conclusion

so precious that children are not allowed to enjoy all areas. They need the freedom to collect interesting stones, leaves, seed-pods and flowers and use them in their play, or for pasting, pressing or decorating their creations — they are natural loose parts.

It is useful for staff to collect objects suitable for different play interests; for example; gardening equipment or cooking utensils and place them into plastic crates for storage. If children are interested in shopping, a collection of shopping bags, plastic fruit and vegetables, scales, paper bags, pens and paper could be stored in a crate labelled 'shopping' until the interest was apparent, along with pretend money either made by the children or plastic play money. A shop could then be set up by the children with the help and support of the staff if necessary and children could play at buying and selling goods.

Older children should have access to these crates and be responsible for packing up and returning them to storage, younger children could help with the packing up but staff may need to supervise the distribution and packing up.

Shaw (in Weinstein & David 1987, p. 210) suggests staff 'seed' a playground before the children arrive so that they discover items of interest, such as a ball near the grassed area, wheelbarrows and spades next to the digging area, watering cans near a convenient tap, all items that may capture the imagination of the children.

It is very important that the timetable allows children long periods of time in the outdoors to explore, experiment and problem-solve, time to construct, develop dramatic play themes, or to socialise in a non-regimented environment. Often children use construction materials to build a home, bus or boat that, once built, is used as a base or part of their dramatic play, all of which cannot be hurried.

Some staff seem confused about their role in the outdoors and tend to hold back from interacting with the children except for safety reasons. It is vital that staff interact with the children in an early childhood setting as children learn through interaction with their environment, adults and other children within that environment.

Davies (1997) carried out a study on teachers in eight preschools to determine staff perceptions of their role in the outdoors and to observe the teachers' behaviour in relation to children's play. Her findings supported the view that staff generally do not see the outdoors as being as important as the indoors when providing an educational program and that outdoors was a place where children should be free to explore and discover for themselves.

However, many early childhood professionals do believe that the role of staff is extremely important in fostering children's development, and that their interaction and support helps the children to make sense of their discoveries, solve problems, overcome fears and misconceptions and learn skills.

Sometimes it will be appropriate to stand back and observe and other times to become actively involved. Staff need to observe the children at play in order to respond appropriately, by offering props, or loose parts that might support the play, extending them by asking questions about their play or discoveries, supplying information or reference books on the subject, fostering a sharing of information. They may even need to change the daily planned activities, stories and songs so that they can support the current play themes and interests. The use of reference books is useful to link the children's discoveries with the printed word. The more the children see print being used by significant adults the more they become interested in reading and the search for knowledge.

Based on their knowledge of the needs and interests of individual children and the group as a whole, staff can provide a diversity of materials in the outdoor environment to cater for the current interests of the children.

The purpose of this book was to provide information that will empower people working with and for children to make informed and appropriate decisions about their children's outdoor play environments. It is not to provide programming details as this would require a whole book to do justice to the subject. However, plans and goals must be set to cater for the children's interests and needs. Programming for the outdoors is as important as for the indoors, to ensure young children grow in confidence, develop skills and gain a better understanding of their world.

Bibliography

Australian Council for Health, Physical Education and Recreation. (1986) *Australian Health and Fitness Survey*. ACPHER National Journal, March.

Australian Standards. *Playground Surfacing* (AS–NZS 4422: 1996). Sydney: Standards House.

Australian Standards. *Playgrounds and Playground Equipment Part 1 — Development, Installation, Inspection, Maintenance and Operation* (AS–NZS 4486: 1997). Sydney: Standards House.

Bernett, F.H. (1911/1999) *The Secret Garden*. Victoria: Penguin Books Australia Ltd.

Berk, L. (1996) *Infants and Children: Prenatal through middle childhood.* 2nd ed. Boston: Allyn & Bacon.

Berry, P. (1993) 'Young Children's Use of Fixed Playground Equipment', *International Play Journal*. Vol 1 No 2 May pp. 115–131 London: Chapman & Hall.

Berry, P. (1999) 'A Walk around Lucy's Garden', *Child's Play — Revisiting Play in Early Childhood Settings*. Editor E.Dau, Sydney: MacLennan & Petty Pty Ltd.

Birkeland, J. (1994) 'Ecofeminist playgardens. A guide to growing greenies organically', *International Play Journal*. Vol 2 No 1 January pp. 49–59.

Bredekamp, S & Copple, C. (Eds) (1997) *Developmentally Appropriate Practice in Early Childhood Programs*, Revised edition, Washington D.C.: National Association for the Education of Young Children.

Bronson, M.B. (1995) *The Right Stuff for Children Birth to 8*, Washington: National Association for the Education of Young Children.

Carroll, L. (1948) *Alice's Adventures in Wonderland and Through the Looking Glass*. Ringwood, Victoria: Penguin Books Australia Ltd.

Copple. C. (Ed) (1995) *The What, Why and How of High Quality Early Childhood Education — A Guide for On-Site Supervision*, Revised Edition, Washington D.C.: National Association for the Education of Young Children.

Creaser, B. (1990a) *Rediscovering Pretend Play*, Australian Early Childhood Resource Booklet No. 4 September, Watson A.C.T.: Australian Early Childhood Association Inc.

Creaser, B. (1990b) *Pretend Play: a Natural Path to Learning*, Australian Early Childhood Resource Booklet No. 5 December, Watson A.C.T.: Australian Early Childhood Association Inc.

Creaser, B. & Dau, E. (Eds) (1996) *The Anti-Bias Approach in Early Childhood*, Sydney Harper Educational Publishers.

Cryer, D. Harms, T and Bourland, B. (1987) *Active Learning for Infants*, University of North Carolina U.S.A.

Cryer, D. Harms, T and Bourland, B. (1987) *Active Learning for Ones*, University of North Carolina U.S.A.

Curriculum Corporation (1994) *Profiles for Australian Schools*, Victoria.

Dattner, R. (1969) *Design for Play*, Cambridge: MIT Press.

Dau, E. (Ed) (1999) *Child's Play*, Sydney: MacLennan & Petty Pty Ltd.

Davies, M. (1997) 'The Teacher's Role in Outdoor Play', *Journal of Australian Research in Early Childhood Education* Vol 1.

Department for Education and Children's Services (1996) *Early Years Literacy Profile*, Adelaide: DECS.

Department of Architecture, University of Queensland. (1977) *Shade for Young Children*. Brisbane: Queensland Health.

Department of Recreation and Sport, Playground Unit (1995) *Playground Manual*, Adelaide.

Early Childhood Voluntary Code Committee, *Plan it Guidelines for Planning Early Childhood Outdoor Supervised Play Environments in New South Wales*, NSW Health, Woollahra Council (no date).

Esbensen, S. (1987) *An Outdoor Classroom*, Michigan: High/Scope Educational Research Foundation.

Englebright-Fox, J & Dempsey. (1996) Swings in the Outdoor Play Environment. *International Play Journal* Vol 4 No 1, pp. 39–49.

Fox, B. (1997). 'Using Fixed Equipment in Primary School Playgrounds — An Exploratory Study, *The Achper Active and Healthy Magazine*, Summer.

Frost, J.L. (1992) *Play & Playscapes*, New York: Delmar Publishers Inc.

Johns, V. (1999) 'Embarking on a Journey: Aboriginal Children and Play', *Child's Play — Revisiting Play in Early Childhood Settings*, Editor E.Dau, Sydney: MacLennan & Petty Pty Ltd.

Jones, E. (1989) 'Inviting Children into the Fun', *Exchange*, December, pp. 15–19.

Jones, E., Reynolds, G. (1992) *The Play's the Thing*, New York: Teachers College Press.

Kritchevsky S., Prescott E., with Walling E. (1977) *Planning Environments for Young Children: Physical Space* 2nd edn. N.A.E.Y.C.

Mason, J. (1982) *The Environment of Play*, New York: Leisure Press.

Mellonie, B & Ingpen, R. (1983) *Lifetimes*, Melbourne: Hill of Content Publishing Co.

Moore, R., Goltsman, S.M., Iacofano, D.S. (Eds) (1992) *Play For All Guidelines*, 2nd edn, California: MIG Communications.

Naylor, H. (1985) 'Outdoor Play and Play Equipment', *Early Child Development and Care* Vol 19 p. 125, Great Britain: Gordon and Breach, Science Publishers Inc, and OPA Ltd.

N.S.W. Health (1998) *Playground Safety*, State Health Publication No (IPU) 9701 20.

Nicholson, S. (1971) 'How Not to Cheat Children: The Theory of Loose Parts', *Landscape Architecture Magazine* 1971 62, 30–33

Noren-Bjorn, E. (1982) *The Impossible Playground*, New York: Leisure Press.

Pedler, H. (Ed) (1988) *Girls and Physical Activity Unit 1*, Woden ACT: Curriculum Development Centre.

Prescott, E. Jones, E. Kritchevsky, S. (1972) *The Day Care Environmental Inventory*. Pasadena California: Pacific Oaks College.

Rijnen, J. (1993) 'Play and Education: A Circle of Growth', *International Play Journal* Vol 1 No 1 Jan 1993, pp. 21–25

Senda, M. (1992) *Design of Children's Play Environments*, New York: McGraw-Hill.

Shore, R. (1997) *Rethinking the Brain: New Insights into Early Development*, New York: Families and Work Institute.

Smilansky, S. (1990) *Socio-dramatic Play — Its Relevance to Behaviour and Achievement in School in Children's Play and Learning*. Eds. Klugman E., and Smilansky S., New York: Teachers College Press.

Steele C., & Nauman M. (1985) 'Infants Play on Outdoor Play Equipment', *When Children Play*, pp. 121–7, Frost J.L. and Sunderlin, S (Eds), Wheaton: Association for Childhood Education International.

Weinstein, C.S. & David, T.G. (1987) *Spaces for Children*, New York: Plenum Press.

White, F., Hargreaves, L., and Newbold, C., (1995) 'The midday playground experiences of five and six year olds: mixed messages and neglected opportunities', School of Education, University of Leicester. U.K. in *International Play Journal* Vol 3, No 3 Sept. pp. 153–167

Wilhelm, Hans (1985) *I'll Always Love You*, Kent U.K: Hodder and Stoughton Children's Books.

Wortham S. & Wortham M. (1989) 'Infant/Toddler Development and Play', *Childhood Education — Annual Theme*, 1989 Vol 65 No 5.

Appendix 1

TABLE OF CHILDREN'S USE OF FIXED PLAY EQUIPMENT

			STAGE 1			STAGE 2	
		All children	Girls	Boys	All children	Girls	Boys
CENTRE A							
Horizontal bars	Number of children	25	11	14	28	10	18
	Average time	1.6	1.8	1.5	2.9	4.1	2.3
Swings	Number of children	20	15	5	22	13	9
	Average time	5.35	6.8	1	3.5	3.3	4
Platforms	Number of children	3	0	3	39	3	36
	Average time	1	0	1	8.2	6	8.4
CENTRE B							
Climbing frame	Number of children	3	1	2	34	20	14
	Average time	2.6	1	3.5	3.4		
Swings	Number of children	24	21	3	26	14	12
	Average time	3.1	3.3	2	4.3	4.2	4.4
Platform with cubby	Number of children	3	1	2	53	18	35
	Average time	2.3	3	2	5.7	6	5.6
CENTRE C							
Turn-over bars	Number of children	4	4	0	0	0	0
	Average time	6.5	6.5	0	0	0	0

		STAGE 1			STAGE 2		
		All children	Girls	Boys	All children	Girls	Boys
Platform in cube	Number of children	4	3	1	10	1	9
	Average time	4.75	4.3	2	7.4	5	7.6
High platform around tree	Number of children	22	4	18	43	7	36
	Average time	2.9	2.5	3	8.2	5.2	8.8
CENTRE D							
Swings	Number of children	16	12	4	20	6	14
	Average time	3.37	3.75	2.2	5	6.1	4.5
Platform with cubby	Number of children	7	2	5	51	27	24
	Average time	5.2	5.5	5.2	7.4	7.4	7.5
Platform with slide	Number of children	15	6	9	31	13	18
	Average time	2.8	3.6	2.2	5.3	4.3	6
CENTRE E							
Combined structure	Number of children	34	23	11	42	22	20
	Average time	5.5	6.1	4.1	4	2.9	5.3
CENTRE F							
Combined structure	Number of children	42	32	10	51	31	20
	Average time	3.1	3.3	2.5	8.3	8	8.7
CENTRE G							
Combined structure	Number of children	51	26	25	59	39	20
	Average time	5.9	6.5	5.36	10	11.5	7.2

Number of children and average time spent by boys and girls in Stage 1 with no adult input and props, and Stage 2 with adult input and the addition of props.

Appendix 2

TABLE OF CHILDREN'S USE OF 'NATURAL' PLAY FEATURES (SAND, SOIL, GRASSED AREAS, GARDENS)

	Number of children	Time	Average time per child	Number of boys	Time	Average time per child	Number of girls	Time	Average time per child
CENTRE A									
Sand	53	579 min	10.9 min	32	329 min	10.2 min	21	250 min	11.9 min
Digging area	12	161 min	13.4 min	10	144 min	14.4 min	2	17 min	8.5 min
Grassed areas	13	181 min	13.9 min	12	161 min	13.4 min	1	20 min	20 min
Bush cubby	17	178 min	10.4 min	14	135 min	9.5 min	3	43 min	14.3 min
Garden	7	51 min	7.2 min	3	34 min	11.3 min	4	17 min	4.2 min
CENTRE B									
Sand	51	669 min	13.1 min	36	501 min	13.9 min	15	168 min	11.2 min
Digging area	21	238 min	11.3 min	6	65 min	10.8 min	15	173 min	11.5 min
Grassed areas	4	80 min	20 min	4	80 min	20 min	0		
Garden	8	42 min	5.3 min	1	3 min	3 min	7	39 min	5.6 min
CENTRE C									
Sand	63	785 min	12.4 min	52	647 min	12.4 min	11	138 min	12.5 min
Digging area	9	1453 min	15.8 min	6	95 min	15.8 min	3	48 min	16 min
Grassed areas	22	232 min	10.5 min	11	93 min	8.4 min	11	139 min	12.6 min
Bush cubby	18	126 min	7 min	4	23 min	5.7 min	14	103 min	7.3 min
Garden	4	62 min	15.5 min	2	40 min	20 min	2	22 min	11 min

CENTRE D									
Sand	70	818 min	11.8 min	51	656 min	12.6 min	19	162 min	8.5 min
Digging area	28	275 min	9.8 min	20	213 min	10.65 min	8	62 min	7.8 min
Grassed areas	49	575 min	11.7 min	32	372 min	11.6 min	17	203 min	11.9 min
Bush cubby	19	189 min	9.9 min	13	134 min	10.3 min	6	55 min	9.1 min
CENTRE E									
Sand	77	1094 min	14.2 min	48	702 min	14.6 min	29	392 min	13.5 min
Digging area	5	16 min	3.2 min	4	15 min	3.8 min	1	1 min	1 min
Grassed areas	24	145 min	6 min	15	104 min	6.9 min	9	41 min	4.6 min
Bush cubby	20	184 min	9.2 min	13	133 min	10.2 min	7	51 min	7.3 min
Garden	14	103 min	7.3 min	5	28 min	5.6 min	9	75 min	8.3 min
Mound	12	63 min	5.3 min	8	50 min	6.3 min	4	13 min	3.3 min

Results of six observations of 20 minutes duration for each play feature with staff interactions and use of props and adjuncts.
Average attendance: 39 children 4–5 years old.

Appendix 3

TABLE OF CHILDREN'S USE OF PLAY PLATFORMS, CUBBYHOUSES AND BUSH CUBBIES

	Number of children	Time spent	Average time per child	Number of boys	Time spent	Average time per child	Number of girls	Time spent	Average time per child
CENTRE A Children on roll: 39									
Play platform	53	503 min	9.8 min	37	343 min	9.8 min	16	160 min	10 min
Cubbyhouse	5	27 min	5.4 min	3	19 min	6.3 min	2	8 min	4 min
Bush cubby	17	178 min	10.4 min	14	135 min	9.5 min	3	43 min	14.3 min
CENTRE B Children on roll: 37									
Play platform	26	299 min	11.5 min	11	164 min	14.9 min	15	135 min	9 min
CENTRE C Children on roll: 37									
Play platform	25	265 min	10.6 min	9	65 min	7.2 min	16	185 min	11.5 min
Bush cubby	18	126 min	7 min	4	23 min	5.7 min	14	103 min	7.3 min
CENTRE D Children on roll: 36									
Cubbyhouse	37	414 min	11.9 min	29	347 min	11.6 min	8	72 min	9 min
Bush cubby	19	189 min	9.9 min	13	134 min	10.3 min	6	55 min	9.1 min
CENTRE E Children on roll: 48									
Bush cubby	20	184 min	9.2 min	13	133 min	10.2 min	7	51 min	7.3 min

Results of six observations of 20 minutes duration.
Average attendance: 39 children between 4–5 yrs old.

Appendix 4

Sun smart information

Reproduced with permission.

Extracts from Information Sheets prepared by the Anti-Cancer Foundation South Australia

Ultraviolet radiation

Ultraviolet radiation is part of sunlight which causes sunburn and skin damage leading to premature ageing and skin cancer.

There are three types of ultraviolet rays, UVA, UVB, UVC.

Naturally occurring UVC does not reach the earth's surface as it is absorbed or scattered in the atmosphere. However, UVC can be produced artificially by arc-welders and sterilising lamps, people working with such equipment should protect themselves. UVA and UVB are the naturally occurring ultraviolet rays (UVR) which are of concern because of their potential to cause skin cancer.

The amount of UVR reaching the earth's surface varies throughout the day. On a cloud-free day, maximum UVR occurs when the sun is directly overhead, at solar noon, 12 midday (1 pm daylight saving time). High levels of UVR also occur during the two hours before and after solar noon. So the danger period for UVR is between 10 am and 2 pm (11 am and 3 pm daylight saving time). These are the hours when skin damage occurs fastest. Damage can also occur before and after these hours — it just takes longer.

Sunscreens

Sunscreens are products which protect the skin against the damaging effects of the sun's ultraviolet (UV) rays. They contain chemicals which either absorb or reflect the UV rays which would otherwise burn and damage the skin

SPF 15 sunscreens filter out 94% of the UVB rays

SPF 30 sunscreens filter out about another 3% of UVB rays.

Sunscreens that are labelled BROAD SPECTRUM also filter out at least 90% of UVA

KEY POINTS ABOUT SUNSCREENS

- No sunscreen offers complete protection against the sun. Hats, clothing and shade should also be used.
- A thick coating of zinc cream does block out the UV totally. It works by reflecting the rays. However, as it is thick and completely coats the skin it is only appropriate for small areas such as noses, ears and lips.
- All brands of Broad Spectrum sunscreen with SPF of at least 15 which comply with the Australian/New Zealand Standard AS/NZS 2604 provide effective protection when applied correctly.

- Using a SPF 30+ rather than a SPF 15 sunscreen halves your risk of sunburn for the same length of time in the sun. SPF 30+ however, should not be used to increase the amount of time you spend in the sun.
- Sunscreens should be applied to clean, dry skin 20 minutes before exposure to the sun.
- Sunscreens can be applied as a moisturiser under make-up.
- Babies under one year old should not be exposed to the direct sun. When taking babies outdoors avoid doing so between 11am and 3pm if possible. Natural protection, that is hats, clothing and shade, is best. However, small amounts of sunscreen can be applied to areas that cannot be protected with clothing.

Hats

Skin cancer rates are higher in Australia than anywhere else in the world with two out of three people developing some form of skin cancer in their life. The major cause of skin cancer is exposure to the ultraviolet rays of the sun over many years. Up to 70% of Australians have detectable sun damage of the skin by the age of 14 years. Research highlights skin protection, particularly in the first 18 years of life, as a major strategy in the fight against skin cancer.

Common sites of skin damage and skin cancer are the neck, ears, temples, lips, face and nose. These areas are constantly exposed to the elements and therefore, generally receive more UVR than other body parts.

Wearing a hat is one strategy that is recommended by the Anti-Cancer Foundation to protect the face, back of the neck and ears from overexposure to UVR. It is recommended that hats are used in combination with other sun protection practices like seeking shade, wearing closely woven clothing with long sleeves and applying SPF 15 (or higher) broad spectrum sunscreens.

The Anti-Cancer Foundation recommends wearing hats that shade the face, back of neck and ears when in the sun. These include broad brimmed and legionnaire hats made of closely woven material. Brims on broad brimmed hats should be 8–10 cm wide. These hats reduce the amount of ultraviolet radiation reaching the face and eyes by up to 50%. Legionnaire style hats should have a flap that meets the sides of the front peak to provide protection to the side of the face.

Index

T

U

V

W

Y